RON FRY

101 GREAT ANSWERS

TO THE

TOUGHEST INTERVIEW QUESTIONS

FOURTH EDITION

CAREER PRESS

FRANKLIN
LAKES, NJ

Copyright © 2000 by Ron Fry

101 GREAT ANSWERS TO THE TOUGHEST INTERVIEW QUESTIONS, 4TH EDITION
Cover design by Lu Rossman
Printed in the U.S.A. by Book-mart Press

To order this title, please call toll-free 1-800-CAREER-1 (NJ and Canada: 201-848-0310) to order using VISA or MasterCard, or for further information on books from Career Press.

The Career Press, Inc., 3 Tice Road, PO Box 687, Franklin Lakes, NJ 07417

Library of Congress Cataloging-in-Publication Data

Fry, Ronald W.
    101 great answers to the toughest interview questions / by Ron Fry.—4th ed.
        p.   cm.
    Includes index.
    ISBN 1-56414-464-X (paper)
    1. Employment interviewing. I. Title: One hundred and one great answers to the toughest interview questions. II. Title.

HF5549.5.I6 F75   1999
650.14—dc21   99-088155

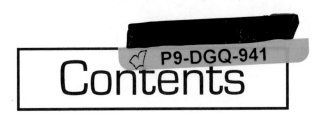

Contents

Introduction

You Can Get There From Here

I t's been nearly a decade since I wrote the first edition of *101 Great Answers to the Toughest Interview Questions*. I certainly couldn't boast of my own interviewing skills before I wrote the book. Far from it—I had often *not* gotten jobs for which I was eminently qualified. So I spent quite a lot of time learning all the mistakes you could possibly make, having made each one of them—twice.

Instead of giving up (which, I admit I felt like doing more than once), I decided to plunge into the interviewing process with even greater gusto. Fortunately—and only after a lot more interviews—I got better. Now, as a veteran of the other side of the desk as well (I've hired hundreds and interviewed thousands), I can tell you that interviewing is more serious business than ever before.

Employers are looking for "self-managing" employees—people who are versatile, confident, and not afraid to roll up their sleeves and get the job done. But you can't get started proving yourself without making it through the interview process.

Let's face it. Interviewing was never easy. But of all the tools in your professional arsenal, your ability to shine in that brief moment in time—your initial interview—can make or break your chances for a second go-around, and, ultimately, dictate whether you're ever given a shot at the job.

Chopsticks, anyone?

Like playing the piano, interviewing takes practice. And practice makes perfect. The hours of personal interviewing experience—the tragedies and the triumphs—as well as my years as an interviewer are the basis for this book. My intention is to spare you many of the indignities I suffered along the way by helping you prepare for the interview of your worst nightmares—at a comfortable distance from the interviewer's glare.

Will you have to answer every question I've included? Certainly not—at least, not in a single interview. But chances are, the questions tomorrow's interviewer *doesn't* ask will be on the tip of the *next* interviewer's tongue. Why? It's a mystery.

Think on your feet

Most interviewers are not trying to torture you for sport. They use tough questions to get right to the heart of specific issues. Their motive is to quickly learn enough about you to make an informed decision—should you stay or should you go? By the same token, if you know what they're looking for, you can craft your answers accordingly (and reduce your own fear and anxiety at the same time).

Is this the ultimate crib sheet? Sort of. But I hope you'll take it a step further and use these questions as the basis for some thoughtful self-exploration. You'll need to be prepared to think for yourself—on your feet, not by the seat of your pants.

An organized layout to get you organized

Chapters 1 and 2 offer a detailed discussion of the work you need to do and the things you need to think about long before you strut into your first interview. Interviewing may not be 99 percent preparation, but it's certainly 50 percent.

In Chapters 3 through 10, we'll get into the meat of the book—the questions for which you must prepare and the answers most interviewers are hoping to hear. (I have not counted every question in this book, from the main ones to the variations, but there are now far more than the 101 still advertised on the cover.) Additionally, I've laid out this new edition in a way that makes it more practical and easy-to-use. Each question is generally followed by a series of three subheadings:

➲ What do they want to hear?
(What information is the interviewer seeking?)

 Green light
(What's a good answer?)   Red light
(What's a lousy answer?)

There may be follow-up questions you should expect or variations an interviewer may substitute after each major question as well.

One, two, three...red light!

The "red lights" after many of the questions indicate answers that will make the average interviewer cringe and the busy interviewer simply suggest you try another firm.

After almost every question in the book, however, I could have included the same list of "general" red lights, those factors that should be avoided in *any* interview or in the answer to *any* question. So as not to unnecessarily clutter up the book, let me just state these all-encompassing negatives right here:

- ⮑ Poor grooming.
- ⮑ Showing up late.
- ⮑ Inappropriate dress.
- ⮑ An answer, good and specific or not, that simply does not answer the question asked.
- ⮑ Defensiveness, especially if it's about something that doesn't appear to need defending.
- ⮑ Lack of knowledge of the company, job, and/or industry (evidence of poor or nonexistent preparation and research).
- ⮑ Dishonesty.
- ⮑ Lack of enthusiasm/interest.
- ⮑ Asking the wrong questions.
- ⮑ Any answer that reveals you are clearly unqualified for the job.
- ⮑ Any disparity between your resume/cover letter and interview answers (such as providing details about jobs not on your resume).
- ⮑ Lack of focus.
- ⮑ Lack of eye contact.
- ⮑ Any negativity, especially in discussing people (your last boss, co-workers).
- ⮑ Inability to take responsibility for failures/weaknesses/ bad decisions/bad results, or taking full credit for what clearly was contributed to by others.

Although most interviewers may not consider any of these an automatic reason for dismissal, an accumulation of two or more may force even the most empathetic to question your suitability. (Some items, of course, such as dishonesty, may well lead to an immediate and heartfelt "thank you...see you.")

Gee, I didn't think you were going to ask *that!*

The questions in this book are grouped by type. They are not in some suggested order. Many of the questions in Chapters 8 or 10, for example, may well be some of the first questions asked in every interview! So read the entire book and prepare for *all* of the questions in *any* order.

I urge you to spend time refining these answers. Polish them until they glitter. Read them over and over again so you become familiar and comfortable with them. Take time to memorize some (don't worry, I'll tell you which ones) so you can repeat them verbatim to the interviewer in a way that sounds spontaneous and enthusiastic—not tired and rehearsed.

A lot of work, you say? It might sound like a daunting challenge right now. But I assure you, by the time you finish this book, you'll actually be looking forward to the challenge of your next job interview.

Pause for self-congratulations

Despite my sterling reputation with employment offices, the first edition of this book became a bestseller. In fact, it continues to sell, year after year. I don't pretend to know why it has done as well as it has, but I will hazard a guess: It's simple, straightforward, practical, and written in a welcoming and humorous style. (Okay, I suppose that counts as four and a half guesses.)

And it has clearly helped literally hundreds of thousands of candidates prepare for every type of interview and every style of interviewer. I'm pleased and proud that this new "millennial" edition will help many more of you in the next century!

Rather than spend a lot more time telling you what you're going to learn, let's just get you started. Good luck.

—Ron Fry
January, 2000

P.S. I almost forgot to mention the usage of gender throughout this book. Instead of being gender-biased, I've chosen to split the difference and mix up the usage of *him* and *her* wherever it doesn't get too cumbersome.

Chapter One

The Product Is *You*

The object of this chapter is to prepare you to comfortably answer one—and *only* one—question: "Who are you?" Believe it or not, the success or failure of many interviews will hinge on your ability to answer this seemingly simple question.

The interviewing process is a kind of sale. In this case, *you* are the product—and the salesperson. If you show up unprepared to talk about your unique features and benefits, you're not likely to motivate an interviewer to "buy."

The sad fact is that many job candidates *are* unprepared to talk about themselves. You may have mailed a gorgeous resume and cover letter. You may be wearing the perfect clothes on the day of the interview. But if you can't convince the interviewer—face to face—that you are the right person for the job, you aren't likely to make the sale.

Too many candidates hesitate after the first open-ended question, then stumble and stutter their way through a disjointed litany of resume "sound bites." Other interviewees recite canned replies that only highlight their memory skills.

I am assuming that, like most people, you are a complex product—made up of a unique blend of abilities, skills, and personal qualities and shaped by your own personal and professional history. Believe me, the time you spend outlining the details of your own life will pay off in interviews, and, ultimately, job offers. This chapter will guide you through the process.

What you should know about you

You may think you already know your life by heart, but you'll be amazed to see how much additional detail you can remember (and ultimately how it will fit together in the context of your next career move) once you write it down.

So, your first step is to imitate the FBI and build a complete "dossier" on yourself. The Data Input Sheets at the end of this chapter will help you organize important, work-related information about yourself. With this information in place, it will be easier to develop a concise and convincing answer to almost any interview question—an answer that will set you apart from the competition. (I've only included one copy of each form. Feel free to reproduce as many as you need.)

Employment Data Input Sheet

Prepare a separate sheet for every full-time and part-time job you have ever held, no matter how short the tenure. Yes, even summer jobs are important here. They demonstrate resourcefulness, responsibility, and initiative—that you were already developing a sense of independence while you were still living at home. Whether you choose to include some, all, or none of these short-term jobs on your resume or to discuss them during your interview is a decision you will make later. For now, write down everything about *every* job. For each employer, include:

➲ Name, address, and telephone number (plus an e-mail address if you have one).

➲ The names of all of your supervisors and, whenever possible, where they can be reached.

➲ Letters of recommendation (especially if they can't be reached).

➲ The exact dates (month and year) you were employed.

For each job, include:

➲ Your specific duties and responsibilities.

➲ Supervisory experience, noting the number of people you managed.

➲ Specific skills required for the job.

➲ Your key accomplishments.

➲ The dates you received promotions.

➲ Any awards, honors, and special recognition you received.

For each part-time job, also include:

➲ The number of hours you worked per week.

Don't write a *book* on each job. But do concentrate on providing *specific data* (volume of work handled, problems solved, dollars saved) to paint a *detailed* picture of your abilities and accomplishments. Believe me, these hard facts will add a powerful punch to your interview presentation. For example:

Duties: Write one or two sentences giving an overview of the tasks you handled in each of the jobs you held. Use numbers as often as possible to demonstrate the scope of your responsibilities. An experienced salesperson might write:

➲ Responsible for managing 120 active accounts in sales territory that contributed $3 million in annual revenues.

➲ Reviewed activity of three telephone salespeople.

Skills: Name the specific skills required to perform your duties—highlighting those that you developed on the job. The same salesperson might write:

➲ Trained other sales staff in new product lines.

➲ Handled telephone support for customer base of 100.

Key accomplishments: This is the place to "brag." But be sure to back up each accomplishment with specifics, including results. For example:

➲ Developed new call-reporting system that increased volume in territory 20 percent within 18 months.

➲ Oversaw computerization of department that helped realize cost savings of 15 percent.

Volunteer Work Data Input Sheet

Having hired hundreds of people during my career, I can assure you that your "after-hours" activities will be considered and weighed by many interviewers. Workaholics rarely make the best employees.

So take some time to make a detailed record of your volunteer pursuits, similar to the one you've just completed for each job you held. For each volunteer organization, include:

➲ Name, address, and telephone number (plus e-mail address, if available).

➲ The name of your supervisor or the director of the organization.

➲ Letter(s) of recommendation.

➲ The exact dates (month and year) of your involvement with the organization.

For each volunteer experience, include:

➲ The approximate number of hours you devoted to the activity each month.

➲ Your specific duties and responsibilities.

➲ Specific skills required.

➲ Accomplishments.

➲ Any awards, honors, and special recognition you received.

Educational Data Input Sheets

If you're a recent college graduate, or if you are still in college, you don't need to rehash your high school experiences. If you have a graduate degree or are a graduate student, however, you should list both graduate and undergraduate course work. If you're still in school and graduation is more than a year away, indicate the number of credits you've earned through the most recent semester completed.

Activities Data Input Sheet

I'm always interested in—and impressed by—candidates who talk about books they've read and activities they enjoy. So make a list of all the sports, clubs, and other activities in which you've participated, inside or outside of school. For each activity, club, or group, include:

➲ Its name and purpose.

➲ Any offices you held; special committees you formed, chaired, or participated in; or specific positions you played.

➲ The duties and responsibilities of each role.

➲ Key accomplishments.

➲ Any awards or honors you received.

Awards and Honors Data Input Sheet

List all the awards and honors you've received from school(s), community groups, church groups, clubs, and so on. You may include awards from prestigious high schools (prep schools or professional schools) even if you're in graduate school or long out of college.

Military Service Data Input Sheet

Many employers are impressed by the maturity of candidates who have served in the armed forces and consider military service excellent management training for many civilian jobs. So if you've served in the armed forces, even for a short time, make sure you can discuss your experiences and how they tie into your professional aspirations. Be sure to include:

➲ Final rank awarded.

➲ Duties and responsibilities.

➲ Citations and awards.

➲ Details on specific training and/or any special schooling.

➲ Special skills developed.

➲ Key accomplishments.

Language Data Input Sheet

Even if you're not applying for a job in the international arena, your ability to read, write, and speak a second language can make you invaluable to employers in an increasing number of research and educational institutions and multinational companies. One year of college Russian won't cut it. But if you spent a year studying in Moscow—and can carry on a conversation like a native—by all means write it down.

Putting it in *your* perspective

Once you've finished completing these forms, you'll have a lot of information—facts—about what you've done and where and with whom you've done it. But any interviewer worth his or her pepper will be looking for more. So once you've finished with the fact-finding, practice putting it all into perspective—your unique, personal perspective, that is. Write down your answers to the following questions, which you should expect an interviewer to be interested in asking:

❶ Which achievements did you enjoy most? Which are you proudest of? Be ready to tell the interviewer how these accomplishments relate to the position at hand.

❷ What mistakes have you made? Why did they occur? How have you learned from them, and what have you done to keep similar things from occurring again?

❸ How well do you interact with authority figures—bosses, teachers, parents?

❹ What are your favorite games and sports? Think about the way you play these games and what that says about you. Are you overly competitive? Do you give up too easily? Are you a good loser—or a bad winner? Do you rise to a challenge or back away from it?

❺ What kinds of people are your friends? Do you associate only with people who are very similar to you? Do you enjoy differences in others—or merely tolerate them? What are some things that have caused you to end friendships? What does this say about you?

❻ If you were to ask a group of friends and acquaintances to describe you, what adjectives would they use? List all of them—the good and the bad. Why would people describe you this way? Are there specific behaviors, skills, achievements, or failures that seem to identify you in the eyes of others? What are they?

What's the point?

By now, you're probably a bit uncomfortable—and wondering, "What's the point of all this soul-searching? After all, I'm just trying to get ready for a job interview!"

The point is this: The better you know yourself, the better you can sell yourself to a prospective employer when you're on the spot in an interview. From your Data Input Sheets, you can compile a list of your best features under the following headings:

➲ My strongest skills.

➲ My greatest areas of knowledge.

➲ My greatest personality strengths.

➲ The things I do best.

➲ My key accomplishments.

Now transform your best features into benefits for your prospective company:

❶ What in my personal inventory will convince this employer that I deserve the position?

❷ What are the strengths, achievements, skills, and areas of knowledge that make me *most* qualified for this position? What in my background should separate me from the herd of other applicants?

By answering some tough questions about the mistakes you have made—and the less-than-positive feedback you've gotten— you can also locate areas that may need improvement. Do you need to develop new skills? Improve your relations with those in authority? If you have been thorough and brutally honest (and it may feel brutal!), you may find out things about yourself that you never knew.

The more time and effort you invest in answering questions like these—while you have a cool head—the less you'll sweat once you're in the interviewer's hot seat. It's up to you.

But before we forge ahead to the first of the questions you're likely to field, let's take a closer look at the interview process itself.

Employment Data Input Sheet

Employer Name: _____

Address: _____

_____

_____

Phone: _____

E-mail: _____

Dates of Employment:_____to _____

Hours Per Week:_____ Salary/Pay: _____

Supervisor's Name & Title: _____

Duties:_____

_____

_____

_____

_____

Skills Utilized: _____

_____

_____

_____

_____

Accomplishments/Honors/Awards: _____

_____

_____

Other Important Information: _____

_____

_____

Volunteer Work Data Input Sheet

Organization Name: _____

Address: _____

_____

_____

Phone: _____

Hours Per Week: _____

Dates of Activity:_____to _____

Supervisor's Name & Title: _____

E-mail: _____

Duties: _____

_____

_____

_____

Skills Utilized: _____

_____

_____

_____

_____

Accomplishments/Honors/Awards: _____

_____

_____

Other Important Information: _____

_____

_____

High School Data Input Sheet

School Name: _____

Address: _____

_____

_____

Phone: _____

Years Attended:_____to _____

Major Studies:_____

_____

_____

GPA/Class Rank: _____

Honors: _____

_____

_____

_____

Important Courses:_____

_____

_____

_____

Other School Data Input Sheet

School Name: _____

Address: _____

_____

_____

Phone: _____

Years Attended:_____to _____

Major Studies:_____

_____

_____

GPA/Class Rank: _____

Honors: _____

_____

_____

_____

Important Courses:_____

_____

_____

_____

College Data Input Sheet

School Name: _____

Address: _____

_____

_____

Phone: _____

Years Attended:_____to _____

Degrees Earned: _____

Major/Minor: _____

_____

GPA/Class Rank: _____

Honors: _____

_____

_____

_____

Important Courses:_____

_____

_____

_____

Graduate School Data Input Sheet

School Name: _____

Address: _____

_____

_____

Phone: _____

Years Attended: _____ to _____

Degrees Earned: _____

Major/Minor: _____

_____

GPA/Class Rank: _____

Honors: _____

_____

_____

_____

Important Courses: _____

_____

_____

_____

Activities Data Input Sheet

Club/Activity:_____

Office(s) Held: _____

Description of Participation: _____

_____

_____

Duties/Responsibilities: _____

_____

_____

Club/Activity:_____

Office(s) Held: _____

Description of Participation: _____

_____

_____

Duties/Responsibilities: _____

_____

Club/Activity:_____

Office(s) Held: _____

Description of Participation: _____

_____

_____

Duties/Responsibilities: _____

_____

_____

Awards & Honors Data Input Sheet

Name of Award, Citation, etc.: _____

From Whom Received: _____

Date: _____

Significance: _____

_____

Other Pertinent Information: _____

_____

_____

Name of Award, Citation, etc.: _____

From Whom Received: _____

Date: _____

Significance: _____

_____

Other Pertinent Information: _____

_____

_____

Name of Award, Citation, etc.: _____

From Whom Received: _____

Date: _____

Significance: _____

_____

Other Pertinent Information: _____

_____

_____

Military Service Data Input Sheet

Branch: _____

Rank (at Discharge): _____

Dates of Service:_____to _____

Duties & Responsibilities: _____

_____

_____

_____

Special Training and/or School Attended: _____

_____

_____

_____

Citations, Awards, etc.: _____

_____

_____

Specific Accomplishments: _____

_____

_____

_____

Language Data Input Sheet

Language: _____

❑ Read   ❑ Write   ❑ Converse

Background (number of years studied, travel, etc.): _____

_____

_____

_____

Language: _____

❑ Read   ❑ Write   ❑ Converse

Background (number of years studied, travel, etc.): _____

_____

_____

_____

Language: _____

❑ Read   ❑ Write   ❑ Converse

Background (number of years studied, travel, etc.): _____

_____

_____

_____

Chapter Two

Take a Walk on the Wild Side

The days of filling out the standard application and chatting your way through one or two interviews are gone. These days, interviewers and hiring managers are reluctant to leave anything to chance. Many have begun to experiment with the latest techniques for data-gathering and analysis. For employers, interviewing has become a full-fledged science.

More employers seem to be looking for a special kind of employee—someone with experience, confidence, and the initiative to learn what he or she needs to know. Someone who requires very little supervision. Someone with a hands-on attitude—from beginning to end.

Because employers can't tell all that from a job application and a handshake, here's what they're making you do:

Pass the test(s). You'll probably have to go through more interviews than your predecessors for the same job—no matter what your level of expertise. Knowledge and experience still give you an inside edge. But these days, you'll need stamina, too. Your honesty, your intelligence, your mental health—even the toxicity of your blood—may be measured before you can be considered fully assessed.

Brave more interviews. You may also have to tiptoe through a mine field of different types of interview situations—and keep your head—to survive as a new hire.

Don't go out and subscribe to a human resources journal. Just do all you can to remain confident and flexible—and ready with your answers. No matter what kind of interview you find yourself in, this approach should carry you through with flying colors.

Let's take a brief, no-consequences tour of the interview circuit.

What (who) are you up against?

There are three predominant interviewing types or styles: the *Telephone Screener*, the *Human Screen*, and the *Manager*. Which is which, and why would someone be considered one or the other? While personal temperament is one factor, the adoption of one or the other style is primarily a function of the interviewer's role in the organization and his or her daily workload.

Let's look at each of these types and how you should approach them.

The Telephone Screener

Telephone screening is an effective tactic used by many interviewers in all three categories. However, people in this first group rely on the strategy as a *primary* means of exploring employment possibilities. For many of these interviewers, the in-person interview is little more than an opportunity to confirm what they feel they've already learned on the phone.

Interviewers who typically fall into this category are entrepreneurs, CEOs, high-level executives, and others short on time and long on vision. Their guiding philosophy could be summed up as: "My time is at a premium, I have a personnel problem to solve, and I don't plan to waste my valuable time talking in person to anybody but the very best."

The Telephone Screener is often the dominant interviewer at small- to mid-sized companies where no formal human resource (or personnel) department exists or where such a department has only recently been created. The primary objective of the Telephone Screener is to *identify reasons to remove you from active consideration* before *scheduling an in-person meeting.*

Among the common reasons for abrupt removal from the Telephone Screener's short list: evidence that there's a disparity between your resume and actual experience, poor verbal communication skills, lack of required technical skills.

Conversations with the oh-so-busy Telephone Screener are often quite abrupt. These people tend to have a lot on their plates.

But what could be better than answering questions from the comfort of your home, right?

Wrong! For starters, you've lost at least two valuable tools you have to work with during in-office interviews: eye contact and body language. You're left with your skills, your resume, and your ability to communicate verbally.

Don't be discouraged. *Always* project a positive image through your voice and your answers. Don't overdo it, but don't let the telephone be your undoing either. If your confidence is flagging, try smiling while you listen and speak. Sure, it might look silly— but it works, and Heather can't see you anyway!

And another important point: You have a right to be pre-pared for any interview. Chances are, the interviewer will call you to set a time for the telephone interview. However, if she wants to plow right into it as soon as you answer the phone, there's nothing wrong with asking if she could call back at a mutually agreeable time. You need to prepare your surroundings for a suc-cessful interview. If the kids are fighting in the background, or you're expecting a package, or call waiting keeps beeping and interrupting, you're in trouble before you start. So don't. Have the interviewer call you back.

The Human Screen

Many human resource and personnel professionals fall into this category. For these people, interviewing is not simply just a once-a-quarter or once-a-month event, but rather a key part of their daily job description. They meet and interview many people, and are more likely than either of the other two categories to consider an exceptional applicant for more than one possible opening within the organization.

A primary objective of the Human Screen is to *develop a strong group of candidates for Managers* (see category three) *to interview in person.* To do this, of course, they must fend off many applicants and callers—a daunting task, because the Hu-man Screen or the department in which he or she works is often the only contact provided in employment advertisements.

Among the most common reasons for removal from the Hu-man Screen's "hot" list are: lack of formal or informal qualifica-tions as outlined in the organization's job description; sudden changes in hiring priorities and personnel requirements; poor performance during the in-person interview itself; and inaction due to the Human Screen's uncertainty about your current status or contact information. That last reason is more common than you might imagine. Human Screens are constantly swamped with phone calls, resumes, and unannounced visits from hopeful applicants. Odds are that despite their best efforts, they sometimes lose track of qualified people.

Human Screens excel at separating the wheat from the chaff. Because they are exposed to a wide variety of candidates on a regular basis, they usually boast more face-to-face interviewing experience than members of the other two groups. Human Screens may be more likely to spot inconsistencies or outright lies on resumes, simply because they've seen so many over the years that they know when a candidate's credentials for a given position don't quite pass the "smell test."

And while interviews with Telephone Screeners or Managers may be rushed to accommodate hectic schedules, Human Screens are generally in a position to spend a comparatively long amount of time with a particularly qualified candidate.

However, these interviewers often do not have direct knowledge of the day-to-day requirements of the job to be filled. They have formal summaries, of course, but they often don't possess the same first-hand familiarity with the skills, temperament, and outlook necessary for success on the job. Typically one step away from the action, they're generally reliant on job postings and experience summaries (often composed by Managers).

If those formal outlines are imperfectly written, and if Human Screens receive no direct input from supervisors on the kinds of people they're looking for, you may be passed through the process even though you're not particularly qualified (or eliminated even though you are).

Not surprisingly, Human Screens often react with a puzzled look when asked by others to offer their "gut reaction" on the merits of a particular candidate. Because they're generally operating at a remove from the work itself, they often prefer quantifying their assessments of candidates in hard numbers: either the candidate *does* have three years, or she *doesn't*. Either she *has* been trained in computer design, or she *hasn't*. Of course, this analysis may overlook important interpersonal issues.

The Manager

This category describes supervisors who choose to (or are required to) fit in-person interviews into their busy working days. Typically, they are interviewing applicants they themselves will oversee; frequently, the interviews are the result of referrals from a Human Screen, or from colleagues and personal contacts.

The primary objective of the Manager is to *evaluate the skills and personal chemistry of the applicant on a first-hand basis*. These interviewers want to get to know everything they can about the people with whom they'll be working closely. (The Telephone Screener, by contrast, may well be an entrepreneur who delegates heavily and interacts only intermittently with new hires.)

Common reasons for being dropped from the Manager's "hot" list include: lack of personal chemistry or rapport with the Manager; poor performance during the interview itself; and the Manager's assessment that you, although qualified and personable, would not fit in well with the team.

Often, these are the people with direct supervisory experience in the area in which the opening has arisen. A Manager who has worked with a number of previous employees who held the same position brings a unique perspective to the proceedings.

Such interviewers often have an excellent intuitive sense of who will (and won't) be likely to perform the job well and achieve a good "fit" with the rest of the work group. On the other hand, it sometimes comes as a surprise to applicants that excellent supervisors can be less than stellar interviewers, but a great many Managers lack any formal training in the art of interviewing.

Of the three categories, this is the group most likely to (mis)use the interview as an opportunity simply to "get to know" more about you—rather than to require specific answers to questions about your background, experience, outlook on work, and interpersonal skills.

Managers, like Telephone Screeners, are often pressed for time. Think back to the last job interview (or series of interviews) you participated in. My guess is that you can quickly categorize one or all of the people you spoke with by means of the preceding categories. This is not to say, for example, that Managers *never* conduct telephone interviews before meeting with prospective employees. Indeed, the telephone interview is a valuable tool that almost all skilled interviewers eventually learn to use, as you'll see in the chapters that follow. But these three models do represent the dominant styles within most organizations.

Time to get up close and personal

There are a number of styles and guiding philosophies when it comes to person-to-person interviews. The overall purpose, of course, is to screen you out if you lack the aptitudes (and attitudes) the company is looking for.

Although experienced interviewers may use more than one strategy, it's essential to know which mode you're in at any given point—and what to do about it. Here's a summary of the methods and objectives of the most common approaches.

The behavioral interview

In this format, you stay in the realm of the known. Your conversations with the interviewer will focus almost exclusively on your past experience as he or she tries to learn more about how you have already behaved in a variety of on-the-job situations. Then he or she will attempt to use this information to extrapolate your future reactions on the job.

How did you handle yourself in some really tight spots? What kinds of on-the-job disasters have you survived? Did you do the right thing? What were the repercussions of your decisions?

Be careful what you say. Every situation you faced was unique in its own way, so be sure to let the interviewer in on specific limitations you had to deal with. Did you lack adequate staff? Support from management? If you made the mistake of plunging in too quickly, say so and admit that you've learned to think things through. Explain what you'd do differently the next time around.

That said, my advice would be to steer away from the specifics of a particular situation and emphasize the personal strengths and expertise you'd feel comfortable bringing to any challenge you're likely to face.

The team interview

Today's organizational hierarchies are becoming flatter. That means that people at every level of a company are more likely to become involved in a variety of projects and tasks—including interviewing you for the job you're after.

How does this happen? That depends on the company. The team interview can range from a pleasant conversation to a torturous interrogation. Typically, you will meet with a group, or "team," of interviewers around a table in a conference room. They may be members of your prospective department or a cross section of employees from throughout the company. (A slightly less stressful variation is the "tag team" approach, in which a single questioner exits and is followed by a different questioner a few minutes (or questions) later.

The hiring manager or someone from human resources may chair an orderly session of question-and-answer—or turn the group loose to shoot questions at you like a firing squad. When it's all over, you'll have to survive the assessment of every member of the group.

Some hiring managers consult with the group after the interview for a "reading" on your performance. Others determine their decision using group consensus. The good news is that you don't have to worry that the subjective opinion of just one person will determine your shot at the job. Say one member of the group thinks you lacked confidence or came across as arrogant. Others in the group may disagree. The interviewer who leveled the criticism will have to defend his or her opinion to the satisfaction of the group—or be shot down.

A group of people is also more likely (but not guaranteed) to ask you a broader range of questions that may uncover and underline your skills and expertise. Just take your time—and treat every member of the team with the same respect and deference you would the hiring manager. And be diplomatic—policies and procedures that you are critical of may be embraced by your peers. Don't blow the interview by offending them.

The stress interview

Formal qualifications are important, but in some jobs, the emotional demands, sudden emergencies, and breakneck pace of work can be downright intimidating—not once in a while, but every day. Even a candidate who knows all the technical moves may wilt under the glare of an etiquette-challenged boss or crumble when inheriting a surrealistically compressed deadline.

When you're interviewing for such a position—whether you're seeking a job as a stockbroker, an air traffic controller, or a prison guard—an interviewer may feel it's not enough to ascertain that you are capable of performing the job under the *best* conditions. He may well try to find out for sure how you will do under the very *worst* conditions. And that's where the stress interview comes in.

Anyone who's been through one of these never forgets it. The stress interview is designed to cut through the veneer of pleasantries to the heart of the matter and see what a candidate is really made of. A common enough question in this setting could sound gruff or rude, which is exactly how it's *supposed* to sound.

I was subjected to a stress interview before I'd ever heard of the technique—which is not the best way to prepare, believe me.

Some years ago, I applied for an editorial position at a major publishing company. I made it past the first hurdle, a screening interview conducted in the corporate office. Next, I was invited to come back to meet the director of personnel, Carrie. After greeting me pleasantly, Carrie led me back to her rather palatial office. We chatted for a few minutes as I settled in. Then everything changed. Suddenly, I was undergoing an interrogation—worthy of the secret police in a country on Amnesty International's Top Ten List.

Assuming that I had been given good reviews by the screening interviewer, I was shocked when Carrie began firing. First she questioned my credentials. Why, she wondered sarcastically, had I majored in liberal arts rather than in something "practical." She demanded to know what in the world made me think that I could edit a magazine (even though I had been doing it quite well for years).

Each successive question skittered in a dizzying new direction. If the first question was about my work experience, the next launched into my fitness routine, and the next, my favorite movie.

Carrie's questions did exactly what I later discovered they were intended to do—they made me feel confused, fearful, and hostile. I behaved badly, I admit. I answered most of her questions in monosyllables, avoiding her eyes.

Needless to say, I was not offered the job. But I did learn some valuable lessons from Carrie that day:

➲ **Never let them see you sweat.** In other words, no matter how stressful the situation, stay calm. Never take your eyes from the interviewer. When he or she finishes asking a question, take a few seconds to compose yourself and then, and only then, answer.

➲ **Recognize the situation for what it is.** It is nothing more than an artificial scenario designed to see how you react under pressure. The interviewer probably has nothing against you personally.

➲ **Don't become despondent.** It's easy to think that the interviewer has taken a strong dislike to you and that your chances for completing the interview process are nil. That's not the case. The stress interview is designed to see if you will become depressed, hostile, or flustered when the going gets tough.

➲ **Watch your tone of voice.** It's easy to become sarcastic during a stress interview, especially if you don't realize what the interviewer is up to.

Lastly, you may well question seeking a job with a company that utilizes such techniques. If they think insulting and belittling you during the interview are effective tools, what's their management philosophy—bread, water, and torture?

The situational interview

"What would happen if everyone else called in sick and...?"

There's nothing quite like the terror of the hypothetical question. Especially when it is a product of the interviewer's rich imagination. We'll talk more about these devils in Chapter 7. But for now, know that the hypothetical question should start a red light flashing in your mind. It's your signal that you are about to undergo an increasingly popular type of interview—the situational interview.

The premise is sound. Present the candidate with situations that might, hypothetically, occur on the job in order to gauge the degree to which he or she demonstrates the traits that will lead to success. It's hard, if not impossible, for you to prepare for these kinds of questions beforehand, which means you have to analyze an unfamiliar problem, on the spot, and develop a strategy to solve it, right then and there.

What most interviewers want to see is a combination of real-world experience, inspired creativity, and the willingness to acknowledge when more information or assistance is in order. (A good many interviewers pose hypothetical questions designed to smoke out people who find it difficult to reach out to other team members for help.) They are seeking someone who not only *can* do the work, but also *will* do the work—and contribute as an effective, motivated member of a team.

But what's good for them is often deadly for you. You will have to devote a great deal of thought to each of these questions. If you find yourself caught in this snare, stay calm and use the homework you have done on your personal inventory to untangle yourself.

The hiring interview

Your first interview with the person who will manage your prospective position is not likely to be a walk in the park. You may be stepping out of the range of the experience and interviewing talent of the human resources professional—into unknown territory.

And you could wander there for a while.

Why? Experienced interviewers are trained to stay in charge of the interview, not let it meander down some dead-end, nonproductive track. There is a predictability to the way they conduct interviews, even when they wield different techniques.

On the other hand, the hiring manager is sure to lack some or all of the screening interviewer's knowledge, experience, and skill—making him or her an unpredictable animal.

The vast majority of corporate managers don't know what it takes to hire the right candidate. Few of them have had formal training in conducting interviews of any kind. To make things worse, most managers feel slightly less comfortable conducting the interview than the nervous candidate sitting across the desk from them!

For example, a manager might decide you are not the right person for the job, without ever realizing that the questions he or she asked were so ambiguous, or so off the mark, that even the perfect candidate could not have returned the "right" answer. No one monitors the performance of the interviewer. And the candidate cannot be a mind reader. So more often than is necessary, otherwise perfectly qualified candidates walk out the door for good simply because the manager failed at the interview!

Foiling the inept interviewer

But that doesn't have to happen to you. You can—and should—be prepared to put your best foot forward, no matter what the manager who is interviewing you does or says. That begins with having the answers to 101 questions at the ready. But it doesn't stop there—the interviewer may not ask any of these questions.

What do you do then? In the chapters that follow, you'll see how you can give even the most dense of managers the feeling that you are the best person for the job.

Simply put, you're a step ahead of the game if you realize at the outset that managers who are interviewing to hire are after more than just facts about your skills and background. They are waiting for something more elusive to hit them, something they themselves may not be able to articulate. They want to feel that somehow you "fit" the organization or department.

Talk about a tough hurdle! But knowing what you're up against is half the battle. Rather than sit back passively and hope for the best, you can help the unskilled interviewer focus on how your unique skills can directly benefit—"fit"—the department or organization using a number of specific examples.

One word of caution: Don't come on so strong that you seem to be waging a campaign. You will come off as overzealous and self-serving. You'll lose. Just keep quietly and confidently underlining the facts (your expertise) and enthusiastically showing (discovering together with the interviewer) how well these "puzzle pieces" seem to fit the job at hand.

In the next chapter—and for the rest of the book—we will explore the hundreds of potential questions you face...and the answers that will help you get the job you want.

How to "ace" any interview

➲ **Relax! Think of it as an adventure.** As opposed to a tribunal, that is. Try to enjoy yourself. Imagine that the interviewer is a sports star, famous author, or movie celebrity you've always admired. (Try to overlook the middle-aged paunch or glaring bald spot.) You'll still be nervous, but you'll be able to focus more on the job and the company. Believe me, that will do wonders to cultivate the interviewer's interest in you.

I'm reminded of a friend who was considering attending law school. Even though he hadn't yet made up his mind, he took the LSAT entrance examination—and scored pretty badly. Undaunted, he immediately signed up to take the exam again. But by the time the next test date rolled around, another career option had his attention.

Even so, he went ahead and took the LSAT again—for the experience (and besides, he'd already paid the fee). This time he doubled his score! He wasn't any more prepared, but his attitude was different. Because he felt very little pressure to ace the test, he relaxed—and performed at his peak.

➲ **Keep smiling.** No matter what. Don't wear a fake grin that will wear down to a grimace. Just maintain a pleasant, relaxed smile that is, hopefully, a by-product of your involvement in an interesting conversation. Put yourself in the interviewer's place. Who wouldn't want to work with such an agreeable person?

➲ **Be enthusiastic.** About the position, your accomplishments, and what you know about the company.

➲ **Be honest.** Don't gush—if you're not genuinely enthusiastic, you'll come across as a phony.

➲ **Make lots of eye contact.** Have you ever known someone who wouldn't look you in the eye? After a while,
you probably started to wonder what that person had
to hide. You don't want your interviewer wondering
anything of the sort. So meet his or her eyes while
you're shaking hands and then frequently throughout
the interview. Don't stare so that you appear glassy-
eyed. Unrelenting eye contact is just as bad as none at
all.

➲ **Remain positive.** In other words, steer away from
negative words as much as possible. As we'll see when
we discuss questions about your previous jobs, you
must learn to put a positive spin on everything, especially loaded issues, such as your reason for leaving a
job, troubled relations with your superiors, and so on.

   Here's a good exercise: Tape-record your answers to
some of the questions in this book—and then write
them down. How many negatives do you find "hidden" in your speech? Scratch them out and replace
them with positive words and phrases. Then memorize
each new answer.

➲ **Don't let an unskilled interviewer trip you up.** Make
sure the confidence and preparation you've worked so
hard for come shining through—especially when a
manager throws you a curve. If need be, your advance preparation should give you the power to take
control of the interview, allowing you to emphasize
the many ways in which you will benefit the prospective employer.

ChapterThree

You're Not Facing Letterman

B ob thinks he's a pretty good interviewer. He has a list of 15 questions he asks every candidate—same questions, same order, every time. He takes notes on their answers, asks an occasional follow-up question. He gives them a chance to ask questions. He's friendly, humorous, and excited about working at Netcorp.com. As he tells every candidate...in detail...for *hours*. Then he wonders why only a small fraction of his hires pan out.

I've never really understood the interviewer who thinks telling the story of his or her life is pertinent. Why do some interviewers do it? Part nervousness, part inexperience, but mostly because they have the mistaken notion they have to sell *you* on the company, rather than the other way around. There *are* occasions when this *may* be necessary—periods of low unemployment, a glut of particular jobs and a dearth of qualified candidates, a candidate who's so desirable the interviewer feels, perhaps correctly, that he or she has to outsell and outbid the competition.

Under most circumstances, as I instruct novice interviewers in *Ask the Right Questions, Hire the Right People* (this book from the other side of the desk), *you* should be expected to carry the conversational load, while the interviewer sits back and decides if he or she is ready to buy what you're selling.

Is it to your benefit to find yourself seated before Mr. Monologue? You might think so. After all, while he's waxing poetic about the new cafeteria, you don't have to worry about inserting your other foot in your mouth. No explaining that last firing or how come you've had four jobs in three months. Nope, just sit back, relax, and try to stay awake.

But I don't believe Mr. M. is doing you any favors. Someone who monopolizes the conversation doesn't give you the opportunity *you* need to "strut your stuff." You may want to avoid leaving a bad impression, but I doubt you want to leave *no* impression at all. As long as you follow the advice in this book and, especially, this chapter, you should welcome the savvy interviewer who asks the open-ended, probing questions *he* needs to identify the right person for the job—the same questions *you* need to convince him it's *you*.

Once upon a time...

 So, tell me a little about yourself.

There it is. The granddaddy of all interview questions. And one that still—unbelievably—makes some of you stumble.

It's really more of a request than a question, but it can put you on the spot like no question can. And if you're unprepared for such an open-ended prelude to the series of standard questions about your skills, background, and aspirations you've been expecting, it can stop you dead and earn you an immediate one-way ticket out of the interview.

Why is this question a favorite of so many interviewers? Many consider it a nice icebreaker, giving them a chance to gauge initial chemistry, get a little insight into the cipher sitting before them (that would be you), and force *you* to do all the talking, for at least a couple of minutes!

Should this time-tested question catch you unprepared? Certainly not. I guarantee that this will be one of the first three questions asked, often the very first one! So what happens if you do hem and haw your way through a disjointed, free-associating discourse that starts somewhere in Mrs. Mahamita's kindergarten class and, 10 minutes later, is just getting into the details of those 12th grade cheerleader tryouts? You may well tie the record for the shortest interview of the week.

Is the interviewer seeking specific clues (key words, body language)? Or, as I have secretly suspected of many an unseasoned interviewer, is she simply looking for the easiest way to get the ball rolling?

It shouldn't matter to you. If you are prepared, you know this can be your golden opportunity to get the ball rolling by demonstrating four of the traits every interviewer is desperately searching for: intelligence, enthusiasm, confidence, and dependability.

So dig out the personal inventory you completed in Chapter 1 (I told you it would be an important prerequisite for making good use of this book) and study the items you listed under these headings:

- ➲ My strongest skills.
- ➲ My greatest areas of knowledge.
- ➲ My greatest personality strengths.
- ➲ The things I do best.
- ➲ My key accomplishments.

What do they want to hear?

From this information, you will now construct a well-thought-out, logically sequenced summary of your experience, skills, talents, and schooling. A plus? If this brief introduction clearly and succinctly ties your experience into the requirements of the position. But be sure to keep it tightly focused—about 250 to 350 words, chock-full of specifics. It should take you no more than two minutes to recite an answer that includes the following information:

- ➲ Brief introduction.
- ➲ Key accomplishments.
- ➲ Key strengths demonstrated by these accomplishments.
- ➲ Importance of these strengths and accomplishments to the prospective employer.
- ➲ Where and how you see yourself developing in the position for which you're applying (tempered with the right amount of self-deprecating humor and modesty).

Again, we're not talking *War and Peace* here. Two-hundred-fifty to 350 words is about right (taking from 90 to 120 seconds to recite).

Green light

Here's how Barb, a recent college graduate applying for an entry-level sales position, answered this question:

"I've always been able to get along with different types of people. I think it's because I'm a good talker and an even better listener. [Modestly introduces herself, while immediately laying claim to the most important skills a good salesperson should have.]

"During my senior year in high school, when I began thinking seriously about which careers I'd be best suited for, sales came to mind almost immediately. In high school and during my summer breaks from college, I worked various part-time jobs at retail outlets. [Demonstrates industriousness and at least some related experience.] *Unlike most of my friends, I actually liked dealing with the public.* [Conveys enthusiasm for selling.]

"However, I also realized that retail had its limitations, so I went on to read about other types of sales positions. I was particularly fascinated by what is usually described as consultative selling. I like the idea of going to a client you have really done your homework on and showing him how your products can help him solve one of his nagging problems, and then following through on that. [Shows interest and enthusiasm for the job.]

"After I wrote a term paper on consultative selling in my senior year of college, I started looking for companies at which I could learn and refine the skills shared by people who are working as account executives. [Shows initiative both in researching the area of consultative selling to write a term paper and in then researching prospective companies.]

"That led me to your company, Mr. Sheldon. I find the prospect of working with companies to increase the energy efficiency of their installations exciting. I've also learned some things about your sales training programs. They sound like they're on the cutting edge. [Gives evidence that she is an enthusiastic self-starter.]

"I guess the only thing I find a little daunting about the prospect of working at Co-generation, Inc., is selling that highly technical equipment without a degree in engineering. By the way, what sort of support does your technical staff lend to the sales effort?" [Demonstrates that she is willing to learn what she doesn't know and closes by deferring to the interviewer's authority. By asking a question the interviewer must answer, Barb has also given herself a little breather. Now the conversational ball sits squarely in the interviewer's court.]

Based on the apparent sincerity and detail of her answers, it's not a bad little "speech" of a mere 253 words, is it?

Following is another good example from a more experienced interviewee. With nearly a decade of experience in his field, Ken is applying for his dream job as a district general manager for a firm that provides maintenance services to commercial and residential properties.

Going in to the interview, he knows he has a couple of strikes against him. First of all, he's already held four jobs, so he's moved around a bit. And he doesn't yet have the management experience required by the job—virtually the equivalent of running a business with revenues of $7 million a year.

But because he has anticipated what might otherwise have been a devastating first interview question—"Tell me something that will help me get a better feel for you than what I get here on the resume" (a slightly aggressive variation on "Tell me about yourself")—Ken is prepared with this winning counterpunch:

"I'm a hard worker who loves this business. I've been an asset to the employers I've had, and my experience would make me an even greater asset to you.

"I think these are the most exciting times that I've ever seen in this business. Sure, there's so much more competition now, and it's harder than ever to get really good help. But all the indications are that more and more companies will outsource their maintenance needs and that more two-income households will require the services that we provide.

"How do we get a bigger share of this business? How do we recruit and train the best personnel? Because they are, after all, the secret of our success. Those are the key challenges managers face in this industry.

"I can help your company meet those challenges. While resumes don't tell the whole story, mine demonstrates that:

"I'm a hard worker. I've had promotions at every company I've worked for.

"I would bring a good perspective to the position because I've been a doer, as well as a supervisor. The people who have worked for me have always respected my judgment, because they know I have a very good understanding of what they do.

"And I have a terrific business sense. I'm great at controlling expenses. I deploy staff efficiently. I'm fair. And I have a knack for getting along with customers.

"I've always admired your company. I must admit I have adopted some of CleanShine's methods and applied them in the companies I've worked for.

"I see now that you're branching into lawn care. I worked for a landscaping business during my high school summers. How is that business going?"

In a mere 278 words, this successful candidate managed to:

➲ *Focus the interviewer only on the* positive *aspects of his resume.* Sure, he has changed jobs. But after this answer, the interviewer is likely to think, "Gee, look at all he's managed to accomplish everywhere he's gone."

➲ *Steer the interview in the direction he wants it to go.* He demonstrated leadership abilities, experience, and a good understanding of the market.

➲ *Introduce just the right amount of humility.* While taking every opportunity to turn the spotlight on his many accomplishments and professional strengths, Ken portrayed himself as a roll-up-the-sleeves type of manager who will be equally at ease with blue-collar workers and the "suits" back at headquarters.

➲ *Turn things back over to the interviewer with a very informed question.*

Although both Ken and Barb rehearsed their speeches, neither memorized them word for word. It's important to remember that the interviewer is not asking you to present a perfect essay, just to talk—person to person. Ken also sprinkled in a little industry jargon here and there, which was entirely appropriate.

 Red light

❶ *Lack of eye contact.* The interviewer is asking this question to find a little "chemistry," so give her the reaction she's looking for.

❷ *Lack of strong, positive phrases and words.* It's the first question and, therefore, your first chance to get off on the right foot. Employ words that convey enthusiasm, responsibility, dedication, and success. If the very first answer is uninspired (especially an answer we all assume has been prepared and even rehearsed), I have almost never seen the interview improve very much. Many interviewers will simply cut their losses and move on to a more promising candidate.

❸ *General, meandering response that fails to cite/high-light specific accomplishments.* It's a plus if you have been savvy enough to "edit" what we all know is a well-rehearsed set speech to ensure that it's relevant to the job at hand. Many interviewers *will* consider it a minus if all they've heard is a bunch of generalities with little or no actual specifics to back them up.

❹ *No relevance to job or company.* Some candidates believe this question is an invitation to discourse on their hobbies, interests, beliefs, and other personal topics. Some interviewers may give you the initial benefit of the doubt, but most will quickly probe for some job-related specifics.

❺ *Lack of enthusiasm.* If you don't seem excited about interviewing for the job, most interviewers will not assume you'll suddenly "get religion" once you're hired.

❻ *Nervousness.* Some people are naturally nervous in the artificial and intimidating atmosphere of an interview, and most experienced interviewers won't consider this an automatic reason to have their secretary buzz them about that "emergency conference." But they'll wonder what may be lurking—a firing, a sexual harassment suit, *some*thing that isn't going to make their day.

❼ *Someone who asks a clarifying question,* such as "What exactly do you want to know?" or "Which particular areas would you like me to talk about?" As I said earlier, I find it hard to believe anyone interviewing for anything has not anticipated that this question will be asked. What do you *think* the interviewer wants to know? Your opinion about Michael Jordan's retirement? She wants to know about your experience, skills, talents, and education, so answer the question, articulately and succinctly, and get ready for what comes next.

Variations

➲ *What makes you special?*

➲ *What five adjectives describe you best?*

➲ *Rate yourself on a scale of one to 10.*

➲ *How would you describe your character?*

Despite the nuances, you should merely edit your "set piece" to respond to each of the above questions in essentially the same way. So although the first and fourth questions appear to be more targeted, all four questions are really looking for the same information.

➲ *Why should I consider you a strong candidate for this position?*

➲ *What's better about you than the other candidates I'm interviewing?*

➲ *What can you do for us that someone else can't?*

These are more aggressive questions, the tone of each a bit more forceful. An interviewer using one of these variations is clearly attempting to make you fully aware that you're on the

Getting ready for the "killer question"

➲ **Complete your personal inventory.** If you bypassed the work in Chapter 1, go back and do it now, before we move on.

➲ **Distill your personal inventory into a compelling opening.** Use specifics to make this a short-and-sweet verbal picture of you, in which you frame yourself as an enthusiastic and competent professional—the ideal candidate for the job.

➲ **Don't memorize it word for word.** You want to sound fresh—not like you're reading from a set of internal cue cards. So know the content. Record yourself speaking it until it sounds sincere but spontaneous.

➲ **Include strong, positive phrases and words.** You want to convey enthusiasm and confidence as well as knowledge and experience. What you don't know, you're eager to learn.

➲ **Use it to set the course of the interview.** Anticipate that the "killer" will surface early in the interview, so be prepared to use it as an opportunity to steer the interview in the direction *you* want it to take. Fine-tune your response to give a positive slant to any potential negatives, such as apparent job-hopping and lack of related experience.

➲ **End with the ball in the interviewer's court.** By ending with a question, you get a much-deserved breather and, once again, demonstrate your involvement and enthusiasm.

hot seat. This may be a matter of his particular style, the introduction to his own brand of stress interview, or just a way to save time by seeing how you respond to pressure right from the get-go.

In one respect, I think phrasing the first question this way *helps* you: He has virtually required that your answer match specific strengths, accomplishments, skills, etc., to job requirements he's already enumerated (in an ad, through personnel, or whatever). You've gotten a bit more "direction" than a simple question like "Tell me about yourself" gives you.

You've also been given a golden opportunity to display the extent of your pre-interview research. And if you haven't *done* any, you may well find yourself in a sea of hot water. The interviewer has set you up, trying to separate the "misqualified" by using a single question. You, for example, may emphasize your ability to meet deadlines and cite specific instances, which clearly shows you worked virtually alone in your last position. In the position for which you're interviewing, the successful candidate may have to coddle and cajole a wide variety of managers in several offices across the country to get input for the documents he is then supposed to produce—and then he will have to follow through by getting each one to sign off on the finished product. Although "tenacity" and "meeting deadlines" may come trippingly off your tongue, the interviewer is seeking a very different— highly diplomatic, team player, etc.—individual. (And, again, that would now *not* be you.)

Tell me more, tell me more

 ### What are your strengths as an employee?

What do they want to hear?

To prepare for this question (as well as the variations just mentioned), pull out those Data Input Sheets you labored over in Chapter 1 and write down the description of the position for which you're interviewing. This will help you clarify each specific job requirement in your mind. Now, match your strengths and accomplishments directly to the requirements of the job.

Say that you have a singular skill for meeting even the most unreasonable deadlines. You are tenacious. Nothing can stop you. If "meeting deadlines" is a key job requirement, be sure to cite two or three pertinent examples from your experience. The more outrageous the deadline and herculean your efforts, the more important it is to bring to the interviewer's attention—at least twice.

Are there any gaps in your qualifications? Probably a few—especially if you're reaching for the challenge at the next level of your career. So now it's time to dig in and deal with the hard questions that you know will follow right on the tail of the ones above.

 How would your best friend (college roommate, favorite professor, favorite boss, mother, family, etc.) describe you?

What do they want to hear?

Personally, I would start with the "best friend" variation if I were interviewing someone. Supposedly, that's who should know you best. So if you presented me with a half-baked picture of yourself, I'd shorten the interview—by about seven-eighths of an hour. Another approach some interviewers prefer is to ask you to describe you best friend and how you differ from one another. This is based on the untested but reasonable theory that if they're your "best" friend, you probably have quite a lot in common. Because you are supposedly describing your best friend, not yourself, some interviewers believe you may inadvertently reveal character insights (read: flaws) you would otherwise like to conceal. So, take pains to describe a person the interviewer would find easy to hire.

All of the other variations on this question may be used by experienced interviewers to hone in on specific times (college, high school, last job) or just to get a fuller picture of you—what your mother or father would say, for example, may give the interviewer a clear illustration of the kind of environment in which you were raised.

Back to the future

 What do you want to be doing five years from now?

What do they want to hear?

Are the company's goals and yours compatible? Are you looking for fast or steady growth in a position the interviewer knows is a virtual dead end? Are you requesting more money than he can ever pay? How have your goals and motivations changed as you have matured and gained work experience? If you've recently become a manager, how has that change affected your future career outlook? If you've realized you need to acquire or hone a particular skill, how and when are you planning to do so?

Green light

Naturally, you want a position of responsibility in your field. But you don't want to give the impression that you're a piranha waiting to feed on the guppies in your new department. So, start humbly:

"Well, ultimately that will depend on my performance on the job, and on the growth and opportunities offered by my employer."

Then toot your own horn a bit:

"I've already demonstrated leadership characteristics in all of the jobs I've held, so I'm very confident that I will take on progressively greater management responsibilities in the future. That suits me fine. I enjoy building a team, developing its goals, and then working to accomplish them. It's very rewarding."

In other words, you want "more"—more responsibility, more people reporting to you, more turf, even more money. A general answer (as above) is okay, but don't be surprised when an interviewer asks the obvious follow-up questions (using the answer to the above question as a guide): "Tell me about the last team you led"; "Tell me about the last project your team undertook"; "What was the most satisfying position you've held, and why?"; "If I told you our growth was phenomenal and you could go as far as your abilities would take you, where would that be, and how quickly?"

Red light

If you answer "your job." Hasn't *everyone* tired of that trite response by now?

If you refuse to offer more than a "general" answer—that is, no real specific goals—no matter how much the interviewer probes for more. Your inability or unwillingness to cite specific, positive goals may give the impression, warranted or not, that you have not taken the time to really think about your future, which makes it impossible for the interviewer to assess whether there's a "fit" between his goals and yours.

If you insist you want to be in the same job for which you're applying (unless it is a dead-end job and the interviewer would be pleased as punch if someone actually stayed longer than three weeks, unlike the last 14 people to hold the position!).

Any answer that reveals unrealistic expectations. A savvy candidate should have some idea of the time it takes to climb the career ladder in a particular industry or even in a company. Someone hoping to go from receptionist to CEO in two years will, of course, scare off most interviewers, but *any* expectations that are far too ambitious could give them pause. If a law school grad, for example, seeks to make partner in four years—when the average for all firms is seven and, for this one, 10—it will make even novice interviewers question the extent and effectiveness of your pre-interview research.

There's nothing wrong with being ambitious and confident beyond all bounds, but a savvy interviewee should temper such boundless expectations during the interview, knowing full well that some candidates do "break the rules" successfully, but most interviewers get a little nervous around people with completely unbridled ambition!

If you have made an interviewer worry that her company couldn't possibly deliver on the promises you seem to want to hear, you can expect a follow-up question: "How soon after you're hired do you think you can contribute to our success?" Even someone with a tremendous amount of pertinent experience knows full well that each company has its own particular ways of doing things and that the learning curve may be days, weeks, or months, depending on circumstances. So any candidate—but especially an overly ambitious young person—who blithely assures an interviewer they'll be productive from day one is cause for concern. The interviewer is really trying to assess, in the case of an inexperienced person, how "trainable" you are, and you've just told him you think you already know it all! Not a good start.

For some reason, some applicants fail to remember that this is an interview, not a conversation in a bar or with friends. As a result, they rattle off some remarkable responses that can only be deemed "fantasies"—to be retired, own their own business, etc.—though why they would think this is an answer pertinent to their job search is beyond me. I would seriously discourage ever answering this question in such a manner.

Variations

➲ *What are your most important long-term goals?*

➲ *Have you recently established any new objectives or goals?*

These questions provide you with an opportunity to demonstrate how your goals and motivations have changed as you've matured and gained valuable work experience. If you've recently become a manager, talk about how that experience has affected your career outlook for the future. If you've realized that you must sharpen a particular skill to continue growing, tell the interviewer what you're doing about it.

Und, zo, Dr. Freud

 If you could change one thing about your personality just by snapping your fingers, what would it be and why?

What do they want to hear?

A savvy candidate will take a trait previously (or now) identified as a weakness (but, if you're really savvy, not a weakness that would ever get in the way of work) and put together a brief answer that indicates awareness and motivation:

"Boy, I had a hard time with procrastination in college. But I licked it because burning the midnight oil all through exam week every semester was driving me nuts.

"I have to confess, I still have the urge to procrastinate. [You might smile disingenuously here.] I wish that I never felt like putting things off, because I know what will happen if I do."

Red light

Identifying a weakness that is job-related or, worse, essential to the job at hand (for example, the inability to work with others when the job at hand is highly team-based).

Citing a weakness that is so basic or stupid that the interviewer has to wonder if that's the *biggest* thing (she *did* say *one* thing) you could change.

Variations

➲ *Tell me about the one thing in your life you're proudest of.*

➲ *Tell me about the worst decision you ever made.*

The former puts you on comfortable turf—a positive question you can answer positively. The latter forces you to turn a negative question into a positive answer, and, because any negative question invites the unwary to descend into a sea of recriminations ("Working for that last jerk, let me tell you!"), it is a potential quagmire.

In both cases, the interviewer is inviting conversation but not as "one way" and open-ended as in earlier questions. These might well be follow-up questions if "Tell me about yourself" or something similar didn't "open everything up" as much as the interviewer hoped it would. You should, therefore, take them as a sign that you've yet to tell the interviewer what he wants to hear.

Dictator or pushover?

 Describe your management philosophy.

What do they want to hear?

Most companies want someone who can demonstrate a desire and ability to delegate, teach, and distribute work—and credit—fairly (unless, of course, the interviewer is an autocratic bastard seeking a mirror image). In general, you probably want to come across as neither a dictator nor a pushover. A successful candidate should convey that he or she has the ability to succeed should opportunity present itself. But they should avoid giving the impression that they're fire-breathing workaholics ready to succeed no matter what (or whom) the cost.

Green light

"More than anything else, I think that management is getting things done through other people. The manager's job is to provide the resources and environment in which people can work effectively. I try to do this by creating teams, judging people solely on the basis of their performance, distributing work fairly, and empowering workers, to the extent possible, to make their own decisions. I've found that this breeds loyalty and inspires hard work."

Red light

One of these wishy-washy answers I've actually heard during interviews:

> *"I try to get people to like me, and then they really work hard for me."*

> *"I guess you could say I'm a real people-person."*

Let's ask Mr. Webster

Q: **What does "success" mean to you?**

What do they want to hear?

You should offer a balanced answer to this question, citing personal as well as professional examples. If your successes are exclusively job-related, an interviewer may wonder if you actually have a life. However, if you blather on about your personal goals and accomplishments, you may seem uncommitted to striving for success on the job.

 Green light

Strike a balance and talk about success in terms such as these:

> *"I have always enjoyed supervising a design team. In fact, I've discovered that I'm better at working with other designers than designing everything myself. Unlike a lot of the people in my field, I'm also able to relate to the requirements of the manufacturing department.*
>
> *"So, I guess I'd say success means working with others to come up with efficient designs that can be up on the assembly line quickly. Of course, the financial rewards of managing a department give me the means to travel during my vacations. That's the thing I love most in my personal life."*

Red light

If the interviewer identifies any of the following problems from your answer, you're already on thin ice and better get back to shore:

➲ Incompatibility of his/her goals and yours.

➲ Lack of focus in your answer.

➲ Too general an answer, with no examples of what success has already been achieved.

➲ Too many personal examples.

➲ Too many job-oriented examples.

Q: What does "failure" mean to you?

What do they want to hear?

A specific example to demonstrate what *you* mean by "failure," *not* a lengthy philosophical discussion more suited to a Bergman film than an interview. This question offers an experienced interviewer the opportunity to delve into mistakes and bad decisions, not a happy topic as far as you're concerned. He is looking for honesty, a clear analysis of what went wrong, a willingness to admit responsibility (with a small plus if it's obvious you're taking responsibility for some aspects that weren't your fault), and the determination to change what caused it (or examples to show how it's already been transformed).

 Green light

"Failure is not getting the job done when I have the means to do so. For example, once I was faced with a huge project. I should have realized at the outset that I didn't have the time. I must have been thinking there were 48 hours in a day! I also didn't have the knowledge I needed to do it correctly. Instead of asking some of the other people in my department for help, I blundered through. That won't ever happen to me again if I can help it!"

Red light

A wishy-washy, nonspecific answer that forces the interviewer to ask more and more follow-up questions to get some sort of handle on what makes you tick.

Always remember why the interviewer is asking you such open-ended questions: to get you talking, hopefully so you reveal more than you would have if he or she had asked a more pointed question. So answer such questions—clearly, succinctly, and specifically—but avoid any temptation to "confess" your many sins.

Tips for convincing the interviewer you're a good catch

- ⊃ **Do your homework.** Find out as much as you can about the company and how the position for which you're interviewing contributes to its goals.

- ⊃ **Demonstrate experience—and exude confidence.** Give the interviewer strong answers using concrete examples that are relevant to the position you are after.

- ⊃ **Be humble.** Convey the impression that you have the ability to succeed, should opportunities present themselves. But avoid giving the impression that you're a fire-breathing workaholic ready to succeed no matter what (or whom) the cost.

- ⊃ **Appear firm, but not dictatorial.** When you talk about your management philosophy, let the interviewer know that you are able to delegate and still keep track of each person's progress.

- ⊃ **Talk about growth.** Tell the interviewer how you've grown in each of the jobs you've held and how your career goals have changed as a result.

- ⊃ **Admit to your failures.** Concentrate on what you learned from past failures, using examples that show how you've changed as a result of them.

- ⊃ **Showcase your successes.** Make sure to position yourself as a professional with a satisfying personal life.

Chapter Four

Why'd You Major in Astrophysics and Minor in Theater?

It's still true. The more work experience you have, the less anyone will care about what you did in college, even if you attended Podunk rather than Princeton. As important as particular courses and extracurricular leadership positions may have been a decade ago, no amount of educational success can take the place of solid, real-world, on-the-job experience.

But if your diploma is so fresh the ink could stain your fingers and your only (summer) job was intimately involved with salad ingredients, then the questions in this chapter are directed to you, the relatively inexperienced candidate facing that age-old Catch-22: You need experience to get the job, but how can you get experience if you can't get a job?

So it's back to "Creative Thinking 101." On your resume and in your interviews, you'll attempt to "upgrade" your experience, no matter how little or minor, while avoiding the temptation to blatantly transform a summer job at the local hot dog stand or on the beach into what sounds like a divisional vice presidency.

How are you going to accomplish this? By concentrating on what the interviewer wants to hear and making sure you give it to him or her. You want to portray yourself as a well-rounded person who, in addition to getting decent grades, demonstrated desirable traits—leadership, team-building, writing, communicating—either through extracurricular activities, internships, and/or part-time work experience. If you weren't a member of many official school clubs or teams, talk about other activities you engaged in during college. Did you work part-time? Tutor other students? Work for extra course credit?

Don't list just a major and minor on your resume; include pertinent courses, too. And a truly savvy candidate will ensure that each resume is custom-produced so the particular courses mesh as closely as possible with the requirements of the job.

What you've been doing—*whatever* you have been doing—should demonstrate a pattern that bears at least some passing relation to the job at hand. What you did during your summers, unless it was a pertinent internship or part-time job, is virtually irrelevant. You *chose* a major, courses, activities—most interviewers will want to know the reasons why you made *those particular choices*. That will reveal to them where your "real" interests lie...no matter what perfect "objective" you've branded onto your resume.

Let's go clubbing

 What extracurricular activities were you involved in?

What do they want to hear?

Most interviewers are seeking a candidate who can illustrate industriousness, not just someone who did enough to eke by. They're expecting enthusiasm, confidence, energy, dependability, honesty. A problem solver. A team player. Someone who's willing to work hard to achieve difficult but worthy goals.

Green light

Activities that bear some relationship to the job/industry (for example, a college newspaper editor applying for a job in newspaper, book, or magazine publishing).

Activities that show a healthy balance. You are probably a top candidate for a wide variety of jobs if you participated in one or more sports *and* a cultural club (chess, theater, etc.) *and* a political club *and* you worked part-time, as opposed to someone whose sole focus was on a sport or cause, no matter how illustrious their athletic or other achievements.

If you're able to demonstrate the ability to manage multiple priorities (let's not forget course-work and maybe a part-time job here) and good time-management skills. Here's a good answer:

"I wish I'd had more time to write for the school paper. Whenever I wasn't studying, I pretty much had to work to pay for college. But I learned a number of things from the jobs I held that most people learn only after they've been in their careers for a while—such as how to work with other people and how to manage my time effectively."

Red light

If you've spent an inordinate amount of time doing things outside of class but your GPA (Grade Point Average) indicates you spent too little time concentrating *in* class. (Anything below a B average should lead you to expect a whole series of follow-up questions, forcing you to explain "why.")

If you have seemingly tried every activity at least once and have demonstrated no clear direction, most interviewers will not assume you'll suddenly change on the job.

Never think a joke is a good answer: "Well, Mr. Johns, I didn't do much more than drink beer on weekends." I'm probably more appreciative of good jokes than the next guy, but an interview is simply the wrong place and the wrong time to play "knock, knock." Even if you're funny, most interviewers will probably question the common sense of anyone who thinks sitting across from their desk applying for a job is a good time and place to test a new stand-up routine.

Variations

➲ *What made you choose those activities?*

➲ *Which ones did you most enjoy? Why?*

➲ *Which ones did you least enjoy? Why?*

➲ *Which ones do you regret not choosing? Why?*

The interviewer posing questions like these is just trying to get a handle on how you think, how you make choices and decisions, and how flexible or inflexible you seem to be in those choices.

What were you thinking?!?

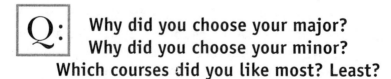

Q: **Why did you choose your major?**
Why did you choose your minor?
Which courses did you like most? Least?

What do they want to hear?

Some interviewers may substitute this series of questions for the ubiquitous "So, tell me about yourself"—your college experience is probably a good measure of "yourself."

If you were a liberal arts major, talk about the skills you developed in some of your courses: writing ability, researching and analytical skills, debating, language and communication skills. Assuming that you took courses related to the job at hand, focus only on those that are career-oriented.

Don't feel handicapped if you majored in something non-technical or non-professional. Most interviewers, even those offering fairly technical jobs, expect to spend an inordinate amount of their time cajoling an endless line of History, English, and French Lit majors to explain how their college education prepared them for a sales/marketing/management/executive position.

What was your thought process? Did you choose a major because it was the easiest? Because it had specific relevance to other interests (as demonstrated by consistent volunteer/work/activities)? Because you analyzed the job market and took courses to prepare for a particular career/industry? Just because it was there?

What other majors or minors did you consider? And why did you choose one and reject the others?

If you are being interviewed for a highly technical job—engineering, science, programming, etc.—the interviewer should reasonably expect that you majored in engineering, chemistry, or computer science, and that your major and even minor coursework is pertinent (with the exception of someone like my friend Andy, who majored in Astrophysics at MIT...and minored in Theater). It will probably be a plus if you demonstrated a particular interest in chemistry or computers or mechanical engineering while still in high school.

Green light

Talk about the skills you developed, especially in courses you didn't necessarily like or want to take. I *like* to hear that a candidate did well in a course she really didn't care for. I seem to spend an inordinate amount of time doing things *I* don't care for, but I still must do them to the best of my ability. When I interview people, I guarantee you I'm seeking someone with the same attitude.

When talking about particular courses, develop answers that focus on the subject, *not* the workload or the professor's personality. Talking about past troubles with an authority figure will introduce a possible negative into your current candidacy. And complaining about too much work is not the best way to impress any prospective boss.

Interviewers don't take kindly to freshly minted graduates who expect to start at a salary higher than their own. So acknowledge that you are well aware that despite your *summa cum laude* credentials, you probably have less job-related knowledge than the senior person in the mailroom. Humility is an attractive trait at times, especially when it's well-deserved: "I know this position has its share of unpleasant duties, but I'm sure everyone who's had this job before me has learned a lot by doing them."

Red light

Blaming a professor, even tangentially, for a bad grade or experience will give many interviewers pause—do you have problems with authority figures?

Complaining about the workload of a course, semester, or year. Interviewers are seeking industriousness, not laziness.

There are interviewers out there—and I'm one of them—who go out of their way to describe in excruciating detail the worst or most mind-numbingly boring aspects of the job. A successful candidate shouldn't be fooled into expressing *any* negative reaction (even a raised eyebrow when "garbage detail" is being discussed!).

Variations

➲ *Why did you change majors? Change minors? Drop that course? Add that course?*

What do they want to hear?

Again, what was the thought process? The change may well be considered a positive—if you explain and justify it well—unless, of course, it clearly was to eliminate a difficult major for an easier one, a stratagem to take more classes with a girlfriend, or something equally superfluous.

If you have changed majors, even more than once, you must be ready to admit that you simply didn't have all the answers when you were 19. (Don't worry, neither did the interviewer.) I suspect many interviewers would find such candor refreshing and realistic. After all, how many high school seniors know that eventually they will (or want to) become accountants, or hospital administrators, or loading dock foremen, or, for that matter, interviewers for human resources? But you should be prepared to show how your other studies contributed to making you the best candidate for the job.

 Why are you applying for a job in a field other than your major?

What do they want to hear?

Life doesn't always turn out according to our plans. Especially when you're young, changes in direction are common. Changes are hard enough to live through without getting grilled about them. But when the interviewer asks about one of your 180-degree turns, you've got to respond.

If you're applying for a retail management position and your degree is in geology, there's a good chance that you'll be asked this question. But count on it—it's not the first time this employer has encountered someone like you. In today's job market, changing careers is common, and there's nothing unique about going into a field other than the one you majored in.

So what do you do? You know you've piqued the employer's interest enough to get an interview, right? So relax and answer the question. Keep it brief and positive: You've reexamined your career goals. You enjoy customer contact, the competitive nature of sales, and the varied management responsibilities required in retail, and you've decided it's the career you want to pursue. And, oh yeah (perhaps with a sheepish grin), there are only 42 new jobs in geology this year—and you didn't get any of them!

Then it may be a good idea to pause and ask, "Have I answered your question?" Give the interviewer an opportunity to express concerns about your qualifications. If he or she does have a concern, be prepared to explain how the skills required in your degree field transfer to the field in which you're seeking employment. You can use the same strategy with your prior work experience. Are there particular things a geologist must learn that directly translate into retail management? Particular skills? I don't know, but *you* certainly better be ready to talk about them.

Just because many students who major in more esoteric areas are, by definition, ill-prepared for some specific jobs, and because many people now change jobs, careers, and even industries more and more, does *not* mean that many interviewers will not make you sell them on how your learning will benefit *them*.

 Q: If you were starting college tomorrow, what courses would you take?

What do they want to hear?

Be prepared to detail changes you would have made in your course selections that would have made you a better candidate for this job. Should you have taken more marketing courses, an accounting course, a statistics seminar? At the same time, don't be afraid to admit that it took you a little while to find the right course of study.

A bit of candor is fine, but avoid offering a dissertation involving a wholesale change of major, minor, and hair color.

Green light

Consider this question a good opportunity to describe how courses that are completely unrelated to this or any other "real world" career nevertheless were valuable in your development.

Red light

Don't claim you would have gone away to school so you could date more.

Don't answer, "Same courses, but this time I'd pass."

Don't answer in a way that clearly implies you don't understand the purpose of the question. You have been given an opportunity to show you know what the job entails and, because of that understanding, to declare you would have taken more pertinent courses while dropping that 17th century Chinese literature course like a hot chop stick.

How I spent my summer vacation

 Q: **What did you learn from the internships on your resume?**

What do they want to hear?

No company really believes that you're going to hit the ground running right out of college or graduate school. Training and experience will be necessary to make you productive. So, as a relatively inexperienced candidate, you can expect an interviewer to do a bit of probing—trying to determine how "trainable" you are.

Stress how the real-world internship experience you've had complemented your academic training. But never pretend that college is where you learned the "Secret of Life." No interviewer is going to react favorably to someone who acts like he or she knows it all.

Green light

If you are able to show how the real internship experience you had complemented your academic training.

Pertinent internships that tie in directly to your new job/career.

Well-thought-out answers that demonstrate consistent career concerns.

Good recommendations from internship supervisors.

Red light

If you sincerely believe—and, worse, actually tell the interviewer—that college is where you learned the "Secret of Life."

No internships in a field in which they are *de rigueur*.

Internship(s) in an unrelated field (especially if it ties in with your courses/activities, indicating that your *real* area of interest lies elsewhere).

Poor or no recommendation from your internship supervisor or a negative reaction from you about its value. (Even if your internship turned out to test nothing more than your coffee-making skills, you should *never* introduce such a negative into the interview.)

Variations

➲   *Why are there no internships on your resume?*

➲   *Would you repeat each of your internships?*

➲   *Why did you pick those particular internships?*

➲   *Why did you feel the need to do an internship?*

Bad grades never really die

 In what courses did you get the worst grades? Why? How do you think that will affect your performance on this job?

What do they want to hear?

Many companies will ask to see copies of your college transcripts if you don't have work experience. So you might as well spill the beans now!

If you flunked every accounting course, you're probably not applying for an accounting job, right? Hopefully, you can blame any bad grades you may have received in some of your electives on the amount of time and effort you were putting into your major.

Do interviewers expect that every interviewee is a straight-A student and, therefore, will have a hard time answering this question? Not in my world. So the answer to the first part of the question is less important than the explanation and how you handle introducing a negative: "Yes, sir, I flunked Statistical Analysis, but it was completely outside my major and, as far as I know, has nothing to do with the job you're offering."

 Green light

If you really can't answer the question because you didn't get any bad grades!

If you satisfactorily explain the one or two less-than-stellar grades. If a poor grade was in an elective course, blame the extra time you spent on your major (in which, of course, you did great). If you blew a single major course, perhaps outside activities were to blame (and you have a ready explanation for placing such activities ahead of good grades).

Red light

Too many Cs and Ds to count.

No reasonable explanation, leading an interviewer to assume that you simply didn't care or aren't all that bright.

A choice that you made based on wisdom most interviewers would question. Although it may have been quite exciting and educational to devote a significant amount of time to getting your friend elected Student Body President, were a plethora of Ds a viable trade-off?

Variations

➲   *Are grades a good measure of ability?*

➲   *Why didn't you get better grades?*

➲   *Why are your grades so erratic?*

➲   *What happened that semester (year) when your grades sunk?*

What do they want to hear?

Again, if your grades were great, you should be suitably proud; if they weren't, hopefully there were mitigating circumstances: work, an unusual opportunity, a family crisis, whatever. But if you fail to take responsibility for a poor performance, most interviewers would consider it a big red light. Whatever you do, don't become defensive. This will lead most interviewers to wonder whether you actually make a choice or simply did something without thinking of the consequences.

Special tips for recent college grads

➲ Don't be afraid to say you'll need help. And when you do need help, make sure that the interviewer knows you'll ask for it. Not many companies are looking for— or expect to find—a 22-year-old know-it-all. If you *are* a 22-year-old know-it-all, keep it to yourself.

➲ Admit that you don't have all the answers. Or begin a lot of your answers with "I think..." or "From what I know about the industry...."

➲ Don't appear squeamish at the idea of going through the school of hard knocks. Tell the interviewer, "Sure, I know this position has its share of unpleasant duties, but I'm sure everyone who's had this job before me has learned a lot by doing them."

There are interviewers out there—and I'm one of them—who go out of their way to describe in excruciating detail the worst or most mind-numbingly boring aspects of the job. Don't be fooled into expressing *any* negative reaction (even a raised eyebrow when "garbage detail" is being discussed!).

➲ If it took awhile for you to find your direction, admit it. Nobody has all the answers at 18 or 19. How many people knew from the start that they wanted to be accountants or hospital administrators? Most interviewers will not be surprised that you changed majors as an undergraduate. Show how your other studies contributed to making you the best candidate.

➲ Don't answer any question about who paid for your educational expenses or about any outstanding educational loans you may be carrying. Go ahead and play up the fact that you received a full academic scholarship or were industrious enough to work your way through school, if you want to. But by law, you don't have to say any more. For more detail on how to recognize and deflect illegal questions, see Chapter 9.

Chapter Five

School, Schmool. Tell Me About Your Work Experience

I t should come as no surprise that most interview questions will focus on your previous work experience. You've bid your alma mater adieu, either last decade or last week, so what have you done out there in the real world? Many employers think that your past is a "prologue" to your future performance. If you do have some deep, dark character flaw, they figure it must have shown up already!

So be prepared to be thoroughly grilled about every job you've ever had, especially the last two or three. And to stay positive through it all.

Let's look at some of the questions you're likely to field.

Life is a Dilbert cartoon

 Tell me about your last three positions. Explain what you did, how you did it,

the people you worked for, and the people you worked with.

What do they want to hear?

Whew! This is a shotgun, in part designed to see how well you organize what could be a lot of data into a brief, coherent overview of three, five, 10, or more years' experience. Interviewers who ask this question, or one like it, are trying to flesh out your resume, catch inconsistencies, create a roadmap for the far more detailed inquiries to follow, and evaluate how well you "edit" your answer to tie in your experience and skills to the requirements of the job at hand.

Green light

If you can boast pertinent experience and skills in a brief, coherent, positive answer.

If you are cognizant of the importance of relating *your* experience and skills to *the interviewer's* job requirements.

A clear pattern *upward:* Increased responsibility, authority, money, subordinates, skill level, and so on.

Red light

Asking the interviewer *my* least favorite question: "What exactly do you want to know?" (Answer: What I just asked for!)

Any answer that is inconsistent with the facts on your resume (dates, duties, titles). You would think no one would refer to a job that doesn't appear on his or her resume, but it happens all the time. (And if you hint at such a problem, here's how a good interviewer will make you sweat: "Your resume says that you were working at ____ during 1996, but you just said you were working at _____. How do you explain that?")

I'll admit to being part of the stupidest interview ever undertaken by an otherwise smart, reasonably experienced person. I spent the first five years after graduating from Princeton trying to be a full-time writer without actually starving to death. The only way to accomplish that was to work a series of short-term, part-time jobs (often two or three at once) while I frantically turned out short stories, newspaper/magazine articles, plays, screenplays, and, eventually, books, some of which I actually got paid for.

How many different jobs did I have? Dozens. Some lasted a day, some months, one nearly two years.

But the only one that appeared on my resume was the two-year stint at a trade association, because my supervisor graciously agreed to back up my "white lie" and allow me to claim that it was full-time—for five years.

Within 10 minutes of sitting down in front of the interviewer for a major magazine company, I was blithely discoursing on what I had learned at two or three of these other jobs. Yes, that's right, the ones that officially didn't exist. I finally realized what I had done, a minute or so after the interviewer had. At about the same time, the interviewer and I both tumbled to the reality—I wasn't getting this job or, for that matter, any other potential job at that magazine company. We parted, amiably, though I felt like a small poodle that had been pulled through one too many mud puddles.

So don't torpedo your candidacy by detailing jobs, responsibilities, and skills that don't "officially" exist. It worked for me!

Don't complain in any way, shape, or form about bosses, subordinates, or co-workers. Most interviewers will fail to be impressed by anyone attempting to blame everyone else for his or her failures. *Even it you weren't at fault,* any transfer of blame will not be deemed a positive.

Most interviewers will grill you about lateral moves (why didn't you get promoted?) and, even more so, clear demotions. You'd better have a very good explanation ready.

If you demonstrate an inability to clearly and concisely answer the question and/or to tie all the experiences into a coherent whole.

Q: What was your favorite job? Why?

What do they want to hear?

The description of the job the interviewer is discussing.

 Green light

Presuming that you have to acknowledge that your favorite job differs from the job at hand in a couple of very specific, perhaps even important ways, you can still recover if you can explain why and how you have changed so that the current job is much more appropriate for you *now*.

Red light

Any answer that inadvertently reveals the kind of job you're really seeking—obviously *not the one being offered*:

"My favorite job was at WNSD radio. It was very loose and informal and there was little supervision, which I really enjoyed. I had the freedom to program my own shows with little or no interference and only had to put

in 20 hours a week to actually get my work done, so the rest of the time I could write or think up new creative ideas."

This sounds like a reasonable answer...if only you weren't applying for a job assisting four high-powered businesspeople who are always on deadline and require 10 hours a week overtime at a highly structured and very rigid old-line firm.

It's not a problem if your last job offered some travel and this one doesn't, or the previous position offered more varied tasks and this one is more highly focused. But it *is* a problem if your answer *fails to take into account what the current job entails,* which will indicate to many interviewers a lack of pre-interview research or the simple inability to realize the importance of matching past experience to his or her needs.

You say potato, I say ogre

 Q: **Tell me about the best/worst boss you ever had.**

What do they want to hear?

Talk about a loaded question! If you're asked to talk about the best boss you ever had, you could try for an on-the-spot description of the hiring manager sitting across the desk from you.

But as a rule of thumb, most companies want to hear that you most enjoyed working for someone who was interested in helping you learn and grow, involved in monitoring your progress, and generous about giving credit when it was due. I hope you've had the chance to work for someone like that!

Now, what do you say about your *worst* boss? Don't get carried away with venomous accusations. They may serve only to introduce doubt about your own competence or ability to get along with other people.

For example, if you level the charge of "favoritism," the interviewer might wonder why your boss liked other employees more than you. If you complain about a boss who was always looking over your shoulder, the interviewer might wonder whether it was because you couldn't be trusted to complete a task accurately, on budget, on time—or all three.

Green light

If you understand that this question offers you an opportunity to accentuate your own experiences, accomplishments, and qualities. There are bad bosses out there, but a savvy candidate should be able to put a supervisor's failures in a positive context. If you say your boss was "stingy with his knowledge," you are accentuating your desire to learn. In the same vein, saying that a manager was "uninvolved" could indicate your desire to work within a cohesive team. Just prepare—and practice—your responses ahead of time.

Red light

Any negativity.

Any attempt to blame the boss for your failures:

"You know, I had to really work hard to learn how to sell spice racks in the South Pacific, but it sure didn't help that my boss had never sold a darn thing to anyone. She seemed to think that everything I did was wrong

and constantly called me out of the field for "evalua-tions." I spent so much time filling out unnecessary reports for her and attending meetings to discuss why I wasn't reaching my unrealistic quota that I never had a chance to succeed. I hope my new boss just leaves me alone."

Q: Looking back now, is there anything you could have done to improve your relationship with that single Simon Legree?

Green light

Of course there is (presuming you are smart enough to grasp the lifesaver the interviewer just flung overboard). The work experience you've had since has shown you how to better accept criticism. Now that you have a better understanding of the pressures your supervisors are under, you can more success-fully anticipate their needs. Use this opportunity to demonstrate your experience, perceptiveness, and maturity.

Red light

"Nah, not with that dumb so-and-so. He reveled in our misery. I'm glad we put sugar in his gas tank!"

The Good, the bad, and the ugly

What were the most memorable accomplishments at your last job? In your career?

What do they want to hear?

Focus on your most recent accomplishments—in your current position or the job you had just prior to this one. But make sure they are relevant to the position for which you're interviewing.

For example, a friend of mine who had been an editor for years answered this question by talking at length about the times she'd been asked to write promotional copy for the marketing department. She was trying to change careers so she deliberately tried to shift the interviewer's attention from her editing experience to her accomplishments as a marketing copywriter.

It's also wise to think about why you were able to achieve these peaks in your career. For example:

"I really stopped to listen to what my customers wanted, rather than just trying to sell them."

"I realized I needed to know a lot more about Subchapter S corporations, so I enrolled in a tax seminar."

This type of response tells the interviewer you give a great deal of thought to how you will reach your goals rather than blindly plunging ahead in their general direction. By letting the interviewer know that you are in the practice of regularly assessing your shortcomings, you show that you are better able to find the means to overcome them.

Red light

Bragging about accomplishments that have nothing to do with the requirements for this job.

Citing (proudly or otherwise) frivolous, meaningless, minor, or dubious accomplishments: "I finally managed to get out of bed every morning and get to work on time"; "I personally raised $25 for the volunteer fire department"; "I successfully typed all my boss's correspondence the same week it was handed to me, even if I had to work all day."

> **Q:** **What is the biggest failure you've had in your career? What steps have you taken to make sure something like that doesn't happen again?**

What do they want to hear?

Before you start spilling your guts, remember that the interviewer is not a priest and you are not in a confessional! In this situation, it would be foolhardy to produce a detailed log of your every shortcoming, misstep, and misdeed. But it would be equally silly to pretend you're perfect and have never experienced failure in the course of your career, education, or life.

So compromise. The best approach is to admit to one weakness or failure—make it a good one!—and then talk about the steps you are taking (or have taken) to make sure that you'll never fail in that way again.

What makes a failure not so bad or a weakness seem acceptable? Good question! Choose any deficiency that might be considered a plus in a slightly different light. For example:

⊃ You have a tendency to take on too much yourself. You're trying to solve this problem by delegating more.

⊃ You're impatient with delays. So you're trying to better understand every step of the process a product must go through so you can anticipate holdups in the future.

⊃ You've realized you're a workaholic. But you're doing your best to remedy your "condition" by reading books on time management.

Try to think of a failure that took place relatively early in your career and/or one that would seem completely unrelated to the work you would be performing for your new employer.

Don't ever admit to any personal quality that might hamper job performance, such as procrastination, laziness, or lack of concentration.

Green light

Acknowledge a failure for which you do not appear to be fully responsible. (When I'm interviewing someone, the way a successful candidate scores the most points is to make it obvious she wasn't fully responsible but is ready, nevertheless, to shoulder all the blame.)

If you must cite a job-related failure, be prepared to convince the interviewer that you now recognize what your error was and offer concrete examples to show how a failure was turned into a success.

Red light

Claiming that you've never failed (unless, of course, you show your ID card from Planet Perfect).

Citing a non-work related failure.

Your failure or inability to offer any evidence that you are prepared to take responsibility for whatever failure is cited nor any proof that any changes were made as a result.

Don't declare, "it can never happen again." This is an unrealistic assessment that will call your judgement into question.

Never confess a huge work-related weakness: "I've always hated my bosses, every one. But I think I'll like you!"

Variations

➲ *What's your greatest weakness?*

➲ *What's the worst decision you ever made?*

➲ *What would you say is the biggest problem you've so far failed to overcome?*

A good interviewer will, based on the answers to questions like those above, continue to probe and put you on the spot, searching for details, details, and more details. If, for example, you say your greatest weakness is a fear of delegating because it always seems you can get it done faster/better yourself, you might be asked, "Tell me about the last time you should have delegated but didn't. What happened? Would you do it that way again? Would you do it differently today?"

Such probing can also help the interviewer assess your character: how you react to stress; how well you handle pressure, failure, or success; your own standards of "success" and "failure"; how willing you are to assume responsibility, especially for decisions or outcomes that weren't your fault; etc.

Have you got what it takes?

 Have you managed people in any of the positions you've held?

What do they want to hear?

Moving up in most companies (and in most careers) means managing people. If you are interviewing for a supervisory position or for a job that typically leads to a management track, the interviewer will try to probe your potential in this area.

So it's best to answer yes to this question, *even if you have never actually managed anyone on the job.* Candidates with experience managing other people are considered more mature, whether or not their subordinates considered them good leaders. What's important is that they earned the confidence of their employers.

If this is you, be sure to give the interviewer specific details on how many people you supervised and in what capacities these people worked.

And if you haven't actually had people reporting to you? You may want to substitute the word "leadership" for "management" and talk about the clubs and other activities in which you "managed" members or volunteers or built consensus within the group. If these experiences have convinced you that you have the right stuff to be a good manager, by all means say so.

Green light

Not just management experience, but managing the same (or a slightly higher) number of people in a similarly sized and directed department or division.

A positive appreciation of the varying skills needed to manage and motivate different types of employees, especially if you never actually managed anyone "on the job."

Red light

No management experience for a job that requires you manage people. (Remember, red light means an answer that may make the interviewer stop and think, not necessarily one that will automatically eliminate you. If companies only hired people who have managed others, how would they ever grow their own stars?)

Any negative expression of management experience. ("Yes, I managed two people at my last firm and let me tell you, they were both overpaid do-nothings!")

Don't give the impression that you underestimate the requirements of management, thinking it's just a move up in position and money but not appreciating the pressures of increased responsibility, new skills needed, etc. And don't appear unwilling to work to acquire them.

They *really* like me!

 Q: **Tell me about the types of people you have trouble getting along with.**

What do they want to hear?

This could be a land mine for a candidate who responds too quickly, saying "pushy, abrasive people" only to find out later that the interviewer is known for being "brusque."

Green light

One person I interviewed gave me what I thought was a good answer to this question:

> *"I was discussing this problem with my boss just the other day. He told me I'm too impatient with slow performers. He told me that the world is filled with 'C,' rather than 'A' or 'B' people, and I expect them all to be great performers. So, I guess I do have trouble with mediocre and poor workers. I don't expect to ever accept poor work, but I'm learning to be more patient."*

Was he *really* discussing this "just the other day?" Did the conversation ever take place? Probably not, but who cares? It's a nice touch! And the answer works, too. Shouldn't any top candidate be impatient with slow performers? He even discussed what he's doing to solve his "problem." Short and sweet, but very much to the point.

Red light

A general, vague answer, supplying little detail, indicates both a lack of analysis and a dearth of self-knowledge. Of course, you don't really want to answer this question—which is why it was asked—but you certainly should know it and its brethren— "What's your greatest weakness?" "Tell me about your worst boss." "Tell me about your greatest failure." —are potentially on the agenda.

Variation

➲ *What types of people have trouble getting along with you?*

What do they want to hear?

If you say "none," the interviewer will assume you're being evasive, stupid, or both. So be ready with an answer. I suggest thinking of an anecdote—a short story that softens with humor the reasons someone disliked you.

A friend of mine remembered back to his first job. Just out of college, he was the first new hire in his department within a state agency in six years. Eager to succeed, he hit the ground running. From day one, he worked twice as fast as his long-term peers, who, needless to say, resented him for it. So his answer was ready-made—and pretty much unverifiable—making it a perfect dodge.

Ready for a curveball?

 Who do you think are our two (or three or five) major competitors?

What do they want to hear?

It doesn't belong in this "group" of questions, but some interviewers like asking this question (or something like it) as early in the process as possible. It will quickly and painfully reveal the depth or shallowness of your pre-interview research. If you clearly have a handle on the company's place in the industry and can adequately, even intelligently, discuss its products, its strengths and weaknesses vs. the competition, the health of the industry, etc., you clearly are a *serious* candidate. Granted, it says absolutely nothing about your particular qualifications for the job, but if you *are* qualified, this display of knowledge may well be that "little extra" that separates you from other qualified (or even slightly *more* qualified) candidates.

Although a lot of hemming, hawing, and nail-biting—along with an obvious lack of an answer—may not automatically lead to your dismissal, I would personally consider it a black mark.

Now *really* tell me about yourself

In the world of business, "style" has little to do with how well you dress (although at some companies, and in some positions, the "right" wardrobe may be a defining element of the culture). Typically, your business style is a measure—and often a subjective measure, at that—of how you conduct or will conduct yourself on the job.

How well do you get along with superiors? Subordinates? Peers? What's your management philosophy? Do you like to work alone or be part of a team? Interviewers will ask these types of questions to assess how you'll act and interact on the job.

And interviewers will undoubtedly base at least some of their hiring decisions on their feelings about each candidate's attitude. In every case, they are assessing how the candidate's style fits in with the organizational culture, their own style, and/or the team's style. So, in general, a "green light" is any answer that will convince the interviewer he or she has found a positive fit, and a "red light" is an answer that reveals differences of style substantive enough to give an interviewer pause. Rather than characterizing an answer as inherently right or wrong, in other words, most interviewers are simply trying to ascertain whether you will get along with Joe or Sally or Jimmy—the other members of the company, department, or team.

Following is a series of "style" questions you should probably expect to be asked somewhere along the way.

 Are you an organized person?

What do they want to hear?

Even if you firmly believe that a neat desk is the sign of a sick mind, talk in detail about the organizational skills that you have developed—time management, project management, needs assessment, delegation—and how those skills have made you more effective.

But don't veer too closely to either extreme. No one wants to hire someone so anal-retentive that he always knows the number of paper clips in his drawer or someone so *dis*organized that they'd be lucky if she remembers it's Monday.

Variations

➲   *Paint me a mental picture of your current office.*

➲   *Describe the top of your desk.*

➲   *Tell me about the first five files in your file cabinet.*

 Do you manage your time well?

What do they want to hear?

I hope you can truthfully say yes, that you are a self-starter and almost never procrastinate. And if you *can't* say it truthfully,

I hope you're smart enough to realize now is not the time to wail about your broken alarm clock—which is why, by the way, you were 15 minutes late for the interview, as you now remind the interviewer. Good employees are able to set goals; prioritize their tasks; and devote adequate, and appropriate, amounts of time to each one.

In answering a rather conceptual question like this one (and what could be more conceptual than time?), try to sprinkle in specifics. Here are a few examples:

"I rarely miss a deadline. When circumstances beyond my control interfere, I make up the time lost as quickly as possible."

"I establish a To-Do list first thing in the morning. Then I add to it—and reprioritize tasks, if necessary—as the day goes on."

"I really like interacting with the people I work with. But when I need to focus on detailed tasks, I make sure to set aside time that will be free of interruptions of any kind, so I can concentrate and work more effectively."

 How do you handle change?

What do they want to hear?

I hope that you are able to say that you handle change well. Business is about change. In order to remain competitive, companies have to adapt to changes in technology, personnel, leadership, business structure, the types of services they deliver, and even the products they produce. And their people need to change just as quickly.

Choose an example of a change you faced that's resulted in something positive. Try to show that you not only accepted change and adapted to it, but flourished:

> *"Recently, my boss decided our company needed to develop a virtual storefront on the World Wide Web. I was given the task, along with a designer, of taking the project from the research phase to operation in eight weeks. I didn't have any special expertise in the area of computers and online communications, so I have to assume I was given the task because I adapt well.*
>
> *"We researched the subject, examined the alternatives, and presented a plan that was accepted. Then I worked with the designer to present information in a medium neither of us had ever worked with before. In our second month online, sales were up 7 percent over the same time last year."*

 How do you go about making important decisions?

What do they want to hear?

By now, you have some sense of the culture of the company you're interested in working for. So shade your answer to match it.

For example, if you want to work for a financial services company, you probably don't want to portray yourself as a manager who makes decisions based on "gut feeling" over hard data. Similarly, if you're auditioning to be an air traffic controller, it's best not to admit that you like to "sleep" on things before making up your mind.

Think in terms of the interviewer's main concerns. Will you need to be analytical? Creative? Willing to call on the expertise of others?

If you are bucking for a management position, you'll also want to take this opportunity to convince the interviewer that your relationship skills have made you management material—or set you on the way to achieving that goal.

You might say something like this:

> *"When I'm faced with an important decision, I ask the advice of others. I try to consider everything. But ultimately, I'm the one who decides. I guess that's why they say, 'It's lonely at the top.' The higher you go in management, the more responsibility you have and the more decisions you have to make by yourself."*

Although this is a nice general answer, you may run into an interviewer who decides to probe to see if the "rubber meets the road," following up with something like, "Okay, tell me about the last important decision you had to make, how you went about making it, and the results you achieved." Can you match in particulars the nice general answer given above? Or do you inadvertently show you do things completely differently (better or worse) than you just said you did?

 ## Do you work well under pressure?

What do they want to hear?

Naturally, everyone will say yes to this question. However, it will be best to provide examples that support your claim to being the Second Coming of Cool Hand Luke. Be sure to choose anecdotes that don't imply that the pressure you've faced has resulted from your own procrastination or failure to anticipate problems.

Variations

⊃ *Tell me about the last time pressure led you to indecision, a poor decision, or a mistake. What would you have done differently? Have you found yourself in a similar situation since? What did you do?*

The questioning pattern I am suggesting you prepare for throughout this book should be apparent by now: Good interviewers will probe, probe, then probe some more. Why? Because they figure you can only rehearse so many generalizations and remember a limited number of "little white lies," so the more detailed their questions, the more likely you will inadvertently reveal any misrepresentations, exaggerations, or omissions.

 Do you anticipate problems well or merely react to them?

What do they want to hear?

All managers panic from time to time. The best learn to protect themselves by anticipating problems that might lie around the bend. For example, one sales manager I know had his staff provide reports on all positive—and negative—budget variances on a weekly basis. By sharing this valuable information with his boss and also with the manufacturing, distribution, and marketing arms of the company, he helped improve product turnover and boost flagging sales. This kind of story is terrific fodder for successful interviews, and the kind of example you should be trying to provide.

Are you a risk-taker or do you prefer to play it safe?

What do they want to hear?

In most cases, the ideal candidate will be a little of both. Interviewers who ask this question are probing for intimations of innovation and creativity. Are you the shepherd or just one of the flock? But they also want to find out whether you might turn into a "loose cannon" who will ignore company policies and be all too ready to lead a fatal cavalry charge.

Again, this is a highly (company) cultural question. The interviewer might personally prefer Stonewall Jackson, CEO, to be leading his troops into battle, but probably wouldn't want him to be Controller.

Variations

➲ *Tell me about the last time you took a risk. Was it the right decision? What would you have done differently?*

If you could start your career over again, what would you do differently?

What do they want to hear?

Interviewers use hypothetical questions to get candidates to think on their feet. They expect you to "know your lines" when it comes to the facts about your career and education. But how will you react when you have to drop your guard and ad lib?

Unless you're shooting for a complete change of career, you must convince the interviewer that you wouldn't change a thing. You love your career and, given the chance, you'd do it all over again.

Feel free to quote Paul Anka (via Sinatra): "Regrets? I've had a few. But all in all, too few to mention." In this case, however, watch which ones you *do* mention and make sure you position them in a way that shows what you've learned. Did you leave your first job because you were too impatient for a promotion, only to realize you hadn't learned all you could have? Did you miss the opportunity to specialize in some area or develop a particular expertise that you should have?

Green light

"My only regret is that I didn't go in this direction sooner. I started my career in editorial, and I enjoyed that. But once I got into marketing, I found I really loved it. Now, I can't wait to get to work every day."

Red light

"I wish I had never gotten into magazine publishing in the first place. But now I guess I'm stuck. And to think, I could have been editing garden books for FernMoor Press...."

Variation

➲ *What was the biggest mistake you ever made when choosing a job?*

 Do you prefer to work by yourself or with others?

What do they want to hear?

Again, the position you're interviewing for will dictate how you should shape your answer. For example, if you're interviewing for a job as an on-the-road, far-corners sales rep, who may develop an unhealthy crush on your rental car but will otherwise interact solely with customers, waitresses, and hotel employees, you won't want to say that you thrive on your relationships with co-workers and can't imagine working without a lot of interaction.

Even if you do like the interaction at work, don't try to paint your environment as a bed of roses without any thorns. You know the old saying: "You can choose your friends, but you can't choose your relatives." That goes for co-workers, too.

Every job situation forces us to get along with people we might not choose to socialize with. But we must get along with them and, quite often, for long stretches of time and under difficult circumstances. Acknowledging this shows strength. Talk about how you've managed to get along with a variety of other people.

Green light

Once I was interviewing candidates for a position managing a production department with 16 employees. Production departments in publishing companies are filled with some of the quirkiest people you'll ever come across, so I had to gauge the interpersonal skills of each applicant very carefully.

After I'd asked one candidate a couple of the questions about his management and communication skills, he gave me a steady look and said:

> *"Look, you know and I know it's not always easy to manage artists and proofreaders. I do my best to convince them of the importance of deadlines and let them know what it costs us when we miss them. I also point out how unfair it is to others in the department, and to the entire operation, when things are held up unnecessarily.*
>
> *"I usually find some way to get along with all of the people in the department, some way to convince them that timeliness and accuracy are absolute musts. It's not always easy. But a lot of times it's fun. When we are rushed because another department is late, I use this as an object lesson. The most important thing is to distribute the work fairly and let everyone know that you expect them to do their share."*

Needless to say, this "right-on" answer won the job.

Variations

➲ *How do you get along with your superior(s)? With your co-workers? With your subordinates?*

What do they want to hear?

The answers to these questions should, first of all, bear some relation to the answers to earlier questions about people with whom you have had trouble or who have had trouble getting along with you. (Consistency, consistency, consistency!) But this is, again, a highly cultural question, and one in which the requirements of the job define the "rightness" of any answer. If you thrive working alone but the interviewer is seeking someone who will always be part of a team, the misfit will be obvious.

 ## How do you generally handle conflict?

What do they want to hear?

"I really don't get angry with other people very often. I'm usually able to work things out or anticipate problems before they occur. When conflicts can't be avoided, I don't back down. But I certainly do try to be reasonable."

Or:

"I've had confrontations with co-workers who weren't holding up their end of a job. I feel that employees owe it to their bosses, customers, and co-workers to do their jobs properly."

 ## How do you behave when you have a problem with a co-worker?

What do they want to hear?

"I had to work with a designer who was obstinate about listening to any of my suggestions. He would answer me in monosyllables and then drag his feet before doing anything I requested. Finally, I said, 'Look, we're both professionals. Neither of us has the right answer all the time. I have noticed that you don't really

like my suggestions. But rather than resist implementing them, why don't we just discuss what you don't like?'

"That worked like a charm. In fact, we eventually became friends."

Variation

➲ *Tell me about the last time you lost your temper.*

 How do you motivate people?

What do they want to hear?

A good answer will note how it "depends on the person," then offer one or two concrete examples. A poor candidate will imply that all people are motivated by the same thing or can be motivated with the same approach, a kind of "one-size-fits-all" philosophy. A savvy interviewer will use this as a follow-up question to "What is your management philosophy?"

Damned if you don't...

Some people have always had a job—in fact, a lot of jobs. And companies are especially cautious about hiring people who have changed jobs repeatedly. Curiously enough, however, many are equally cautious about hiring people who have never moved. If either of these situations describes your particular job history, here's how to handle it.

You've changed jobs quite frequently. How do we know you'll stick around?

What do they want to hear?

The hiring process is expensive for companies and is time-consuming for managers. Job-hoppers only serve to make it a more frequent process. So, in framing your reply, convince the interviewer you have staying power by painting the position on offer as your career's "Promised Land."

 ### Green light

Take one of these two approaches:

❶ Confess that you had some difficulty defining your career goals at first, but now you are quite sure of your direction.

❷ Convince the interviewer that you left previous positions only after you realized that moving on was the only way to increase your responsibilities and broaden your experience.

Be sure to emphasize the fact that you would like nothing better than to stay and grow with a company. Here's an example to study if you have to explain your own job-hopping history.

Sherri had four jobs in the first six years after college graduation. Her clever reply to an interviewer's skepticism about her staying power combines both techniques:

"All through college, I was convinced that I wanted to be a programmer. But after a few months in my first job, I found that I was unhappy. Naturally, I blamed the

company and the job. So when an opportunity opened up at Lakeside Bank, I grabbed it. But not long after the initial euphoria wore off, I was unhappy again.

"By this time I'd noticed that I really did enjoy the part of my job that dealt with applications. So when I heard about the job in end-user computing at SafeInvest, I went for it. I learned a lot there, until I hit a 'glass ceiling.' It was a small firm, so there was no place for me to grow.

"I was recruited for the applications position at Deep Pockets Bank, and I got the job because of some of the innovations I'd developed at SI. The work has been terrific. But once again, I find that I'm a one-person department.

"This position offers the opportunity to manage a department and interact with programmers and applications specialists on the cutting edge of technology. Throughout my career, the one thing that has remained constant is my love of learning. This job would give me the chance to learn so much."

Variation

➲ *You've been with your current employer for only a short amount of time. Is this an indication that you'll be moving around a lot throughout your career?*

...And damned if you do

 You've been with the same organization for __ years. Won't you have a tough time getting used to a new culture, company, atmosphere, team, etc.?

What do they want to hear?

The flip side of the previous question. Here's what the interviewer is doing to you: If you've moved around, she questions your staying power. If you stuck with a single company, she questions your initiative. Lose-lose.

Here's how to fight back: During your tenure with your current company, you've probably worked for more than one boss. You may even have supervised many different types of people in various departments. Certainly you've teamed up with a variety of co-workers. And from inside this one organization, you've had a chance to observe a wide variety of other organizations—competitors, vendors, customers, and so on. Get it?

You're flexible—and loyal. You should remind the interviewer that this can prove a valuable combination.

By the time you've been asked introductory questions, questions about high school and college experiences, and these preliminary "on-the-job" questions, you should certainly have an idea of whether you are still a viable candidate. And if you are, you can expect even more questions. (If you are not, you may politely be led to the door any time now.)

If the interviewer is still unsure, it's time for her to ask even more detailed questions. She's invited you to paint her a picture. Okay, Rembrandt, what else do you have to offer her?

Tips for handling questions about work

➲ **Be honest.** But play up your strengths and whitewash your weaknesses. If you have to talk about negative experiences, point out what you learned from them and why you wouldn't make the same mistakes again.

➲ **Introduce only the positive.** Don't give away information that could come back to haunt you.

➲ **Strike a balance between portraying yourself as a "company man or woman" and a "loose cannon."** Screening interviewers and hiring managers are often attracted to risk-takers. But they also put a lot of stock in playing by the rules. Your pre-interview research should clarify which road to take. If in doubt, choose neither—settle for a balanced reply.

➲ **Use specific work situations to illustrate your points.** If you sense the interview drifting into subjectivity, plan to bring the interviewer back by using concrete examples from your past experience. Don't just say you're organized. Tell how you organized a complex project from beginning to end. Remember, insofar as possible, you want the interviewer basing his or her decision on the *facts*—your strengths, qualifications, and accomplishments—not some subjective evaluation of "chemistry."

➲ **Choose your words carefully.** Make sure that you are indeed answering questions and not suggesting other areas the interviewer hadn't thought to explore. For example, I suggest, "I'm looking for greater challenges," rather than, "The boss didn't give me enough to do." Do you really want to travel down *that* road?

Chapter Six

Let's Focus on Some Specifics

Now that the generalities have been covered—pesky things such as motivation and your basic on-the-job attitude—good interviewers will try to glean even more particular information on your past performance. Take heart—if you've made it this far, you're still a viable candidate!

Choose one from column A...

Tell me about the last time you:

- ➲ Made a mistake.
- ➲ Made a good decision.
- ➲ Made a poor decision.
- ➲ Fired someone.
- ➲ Hired someone.
- ➲ Failed to complete a project on time.
- ➲ Found a unique solution to a problem.
- ➲ Found a creative solution to a problem.

- Found a cost-effective solution to a problem.
- Aimed too high.
- Aimed too low.
- Made (or lost) a great sale.
- Saved the company money.
- Went over budget.

What do they want to hear?

These are "open-ended" questions like "Tell me about yourself," thus encouraging you to talk but clearly requiring focused, specific answers. Follow-up questions should be obvious based on your initial answer: "Okay, I understand how the lack of divisional coordination led to the budget shortfall. And you have clearly taken responsibility for your part in the miscommunication. But what did you do to change procedures to ensure it didn't happen again? And, by the way, *did* it happen again?"

Expect a seasoned interviewer to keep probing and asking for more specifics, more examples, who said what, who did what, what were the results, what would you do differently now, what do you need to change to do better in the future, what *have* you changed, etc.

Green light

A *specific* answer to a *specific* question, the more detailed the better.

An answer to any of the above questions that has a beginning, middle, and an end, much like a good story: Here's what happened, here's what I did, here's what I learned.

Some of the questions *require* job-related answers; others may allow for examples chosen from outside activities, perhaps volunteer work, or any part of one's personal life. A savvy candidate will "mix and match" stories and examples to convince an interviewer she is well-rounded and actually has a life after 5 p.m.

Take appropriate credit for an accomplishment (reducing costs, increasing revenues, a creative solution, a tough sale) but be fair and honest enough to put your own contribution within the context of what your team/organization/boss/assistants did...and try to appear to be bending over backwards to do so.

Most interviewers will favor a candidate who has been around long enough to make good *and* bad decisions, good *and* bad hires, good and bad *choices*. The breadth of your exposure to the basic tenets of business is more important to *me*, anyway, than the extent of your experience.

Red light

Avoid giving the impression you're a "hard-working, self-starting, high-energy" Mr. Generalization who can't furnish an interviewer with too many examples of your wonderfulness, no matter how many questions she tosses you.

Most interviewers will be suspicious of someone with years of experience in the same job who seems to have enjoyed little exposure to the normal day-to-day vagaries of the world. You hired someone once and they were fine. Never fired anyone. Can't remember the last time you actually had to make a major decision.

No matter how talented you are (or think you are), avoid claiming to have been CEO/COO/CFO/Creative Star/Sales Guru—all at the same time. Even if you are a prodigy who would give Mozart pause, you should be savvy enough not to take credit for every success your company achieved in the last decade (especially if you've only been there three years!).

I always found it interesting, for example, that seven different independent publicists approached me at a trade show and that every single one of them claimed—in their literature and even on their business cards—to be totally responsible for the success of the book, *Chicken Soup for the Soul*. While I'm not sure every one of them had even worked on the book, clearly not every one of them was singularly in charge of the publicity plan!

...And one from column B

What do you do when you're having trouble...

- ➲ Solving a problem?
- ➲ With a subordinate?
- ➲ With a boss?
- ➲ With your job?

What do you do when...

- ➲ Things are slow?
- ➲ Things are hectic?
- ➲ You're burned out?
- ➲ You have multiple priorities (family/work/school, etc.)?

What do they want to hear?

These questions are just further attempts to figure out how you think and act in reality. You may well have been asked about problems with a boss, co-workers, etc., 10 minutes or 30 minutes before, so be careful—a good interviewer may be trying to trip you up by honing in on the same issue from a different direction. The style of question framed along the lines of "What do you do when..." is very different from "Do you have problem with __?"

What are the skills you most need to acquire/develop to advance your career?

What do they want to hear?

You should claim to be developing a skill in line with the job for which you're interviewing, otherwise why are you talking about it? "Well, I really need to grip my tennis racquet more firmly at the net. My stroke is just all wrong." *Oookay.*

Let me rephrase that:

 What do your supervisors tend to criticize most about your performance?

What do they want to hear?

This is another way of framing a series of questions you've probably already been asked: What's your greatest weakness? What was your greatest failure? What would your supervisor say about you?

By asking what amounts to the same question three or four different ways, it gives a seasoned interviewer the ability to look for the inconsistencies that you might well reveal.

Green light

You should certainly assume your references will be checked—and your current supervisor contacted—so your answer better match what your supervisor says.

Consider discussing an evaluation from an earlier job, switching to what you did about it and claiming that your current supervisor would, therefore, not consider it a problem any longer. This is a really beautiful answer because it's possible that the interviewer can't really check the initial evaluation, which makes the rest of the scenario moot, but it works for you!

Just remember: A good interviewer will find a way to get around this elegant subterfuge: "Was there anything your current supervisor criticized you for in your last performance evaluation?" or "What specific areas did your current supervisor's last evaluation indicate you needed to work on?"

 Red light

Never cite a personal quality that might hamper (or convince the interviewer that it might) your job performance, such as procrastination, laziness, lack of concentration, a hot temper, or tardiness.

Most interviewers probably will be suspicious if you claim never to have received a poor evaluation. While not necessarily untrue—there are companies and bosses that fail to do systematic evaluations or fail to take them very seriously—it will probably just lead you to this follow-up question: "Tell me about the last time your boss criticized you. What for? What was your response? What have you done to fix/solve/change what he criticized?" I *would* find it highly suspect for any candidate to claim they have never ever been called on the carpet for *any*thing.

If you're so brilliant, why aren't you rich?

Q: **Did you inaugurate new procedures (systems, policies, etc.) in your previous position? Tell me about them.**

What do they want to hear?

Of course! You had some very good solutions you'd be happy to share with the interviewer. Regrettably, however, some (or none?) could be implemented because of circumstances beyond your control.

You don't have to be a divisional president or department head to answer this question. An administrative assistant may have creatively and by his or her own volition instituted a new filing system or a better way to delegate departmental correspondence, or simply utilized technology to improve a mundane task, like keeping the boss's calendar.

The interviewer is seeking industriousness, creativity, caring about the organization and its success. So this is the time to bring up those facts and figures we talked about earlier. Describe the changes or improvements you were responsible for making and identify how they helped the company, in terms of increased profits, cost savings, or improved production.

Variation

➲ *Was there anything your company (or department or team) could have done to be more successful?*

Here's a perfectly acceptable answer:

"Sure, we could have expanded our product line, perhaps even doubled it, to take advantage of our superior distribution. But we just didn't have the capital and couldn't get the financing."

Have you been in charge of budgeting, approving expenses, and monitoring departmental progress against financial goals? Are you very qualified in this area?

What do they want to hear?

Again, financial responsibility signals an employer's faith in you. If you haven't had many—or any—fiscal duties, admit it. But as always, nothing is stopping you from being creative in the way you frame your reply. Here's an example:

> *"Well, I've never actually run a department, but I've had to set and meet budgetary goals for several projects I've worked on. In fact, I did this so often that I took a class to learn how to set up and use Microsoft Excel spreadsheets."*

If you've had broader responsibilities, talk about your approval authority. What is the largest expenditure you could sign off on? Let the interviewer know, in round numbers, the income and expenses of the departments you've supervised.

Be careful. This question is also designed to trap you if you lied to the previous question. "Managed 14 people but had no financial responsibilities at all? Hmmm."

If you answer this question *positively*, expect more probing: "In your experience, what are the most common obstacles you've faced when completing assignments or projects on time and on budget? Give me one or two examples and how you dealt with them."

Hiring and firing and cash, oh my!

 : Have you ever fired anyone? Why?

What do they want to hear?

Even if you had good reason, you know that firing someone is never pleasant. Say so, and provide a "sanitized" (and brief!) version of the events to the interviewer. Remember, you don't want to seem like a negative person, one who might disrupt an entire department, nor appear *too* empathetic.

You should express a modicum of sympathy for the person (people) who got the axe (you clearly didn't relish your role), an understanding that sometimes people have to be fired (but business is business), and a readiness to do it appropriately, professionally, and compassionately, when required.

Green light

Let's say you fired someone for not meeting productivity goals. You might be thinking, "Boy, I'm glad I got rid of that bum. He was nothing but a wimp and whiner who never did a good day's work in all the time he was on the job." Go ahead and *think* that. But when you open your mouth, *say* something like this:

> *"Yes, I fired someone who continually fell short of his productivity goals. His shortcomings were documented and discussed with him over a period of months. But in that time he failed to show any real improvement. I had no choice. As a supervisor, I want everyone in my department to work out. Let's face it, though, not everyone is equally dedicated to his or her job."*

If you haven't actually fired anyone, here is one way to respond:

"I've never actually fired anyone myself, but it was the policy at my company that no hirings or firings should be unilateral. I was asked on two occasions to give my opinion about someone else's performance. It's never easy to be honest about a co-worker's shortcomings. But I felt I had to do what was best for the department and fair to everyone else in it."

Have you ever hired anyone? Why did you choose them?

What do they want to hear?

If you have hired one or more people during your career, your answer might go something like this:

"Yes, I have hired people. I have also decided whether some internal applicants were right for jobs in my department. The first time I hired someone, I concentrated on checking off all the right qualifications. I just went down a checklist.

"Since then, though, I've learned that some candidates who became excellent workers didn't necessarily have every qualification on that checklist. They more than make up for what they lacked in the beginning with enthusiasm and a willingness to work with others."

What if you've never hired anyone? Show the interviewer you appreciate that he or she is trying to evaluate both your management potential and "people" skills, and try something like this:

"Not really. But on several occasions I was asked to speak to prospective applicants and offer my opinion. Of course, in those cases, I was trying to determine whether that person would be a team player and if he or she would get along with the other people in the department."

Let's take it from the top

If you're seeking an executive-level position, most of the previous questions in this book are just as pertinent as if you were interviewing to be a receptionist (although the interviewer would expect a different level of answer!). Here are a few questions you can expect if you are a potential CFO, CIO, or Executive Vice President:

Tell me about the last situation in which you were directed to overhaul a problem unit/department/division/company.

What were you confronted with, what did you do, what kind of culture did you attempt to create?

How many people did you hire and fire?

What goals did you establish?

How long was your outlook and what were the results?

What do they want to hear?

Every question is designed to get a handle on your management philosophy; ability to conceptualize on a general basis and to implement on a specific one; ability to create loyalty, unity, shared goals; ability to create and produce under pressure; ability to stay within budget and/or produce over budget; and so on.

 How do you "stay in the loop"?

What do they want to hear?

There are many ways to get the information an interviewer is seeking with this question. Here are some variations:

➲ *How many meetings do you schedule/ attend per week/month?*

➲ *Are you a MBWA (Management by Walking Around) afficionado?*

➲ *Do you spend a lot of time in your subordinates' offices asking questions or do you prefer to wait for them to come to you with problems?*

All of the above are much more specific than "Explain your management philosophy," a question an experienced interviewee can wiggle through with a couple of business-guru quotes. The more senior your current position—and the more "executive" the position for which you're applying—the more likely these types of questions will be asked. And the more important the answers to them will be.

How do you deal with subordinates who are becoming part of the problem rather than part of the solution?

What do they want to hear?

This has been asked previously in other forms. The interviewer is trying to separate the real leaders from the "managers with a title" and to ascertain whether your particular style will mesh with the organization's.

 See that picture frame on the wall? Sell it to me.

Or the pen, the desk, the paperweight, whatever. I'm not sure I particularly like this question—although it isn't one that should surprise an entry-level sales candidate—and I'm not really sure where to talk about it, so I guess this is as good a place as any.

What do they want to hear?

One of the major characteristics of a truly good salesperson is his or her ability to ask questions and listen to the answers (kind of like a really good interviewer). So a good sales candidate will begin by asking a series of questions about the object and about the interviewer's particular needs.

An old friend of mine, a sales superstar, once told me that if he asked enough questions, and asked enough of the *right* questions, sooner or later every prospect would tell him exactly what he needed to say to get the sale.

Obviously, the ultimate test of a sales candidate is whether he or she is really capable of selling that object to the interviewer. What about the candidate who will have nothing to do with sales? Some interviewers may still consider this a viable question if only to see how you react under pressure. The less sales-oriented you are, the more this question may bother you.

More tips for answering questions about work

⊃ **Be positive about your reasons for leaving your current job.** Or any previous jobs, for that matter. The key word to remember is "more." You want *more* responsibility, *more* challenges, *more* opportunity and finally (but don't play this up, except as a natural consequence of the previous "mores"), *more* money.

⊃ **If you've been fired, stress what you learned from the experience.** Be as positive as you can.

⊃ **Quantify the confidence other employers have placed in you.** Do this by stressing specific facts, figures, and measurable accomplishments. Mention the number of employees you've supervised, the amount of money you controlled, the earnings that your department achieved under your management.

⊃ **Never speak badly of past supervisors or employers.** It's the biggest negative of all, and you're highlighting nothing but the positive, right?

⊃ **Make the job you're interviewing for your chief objective.** Frame your answers so that you let the interviewer know that you see this job as a means to achieving your ultimate career objectives. Be careful not to make it sound like either a stepping stone or a safe haven.

Chapter Seven

Let's Look at Your Current (Last) Job, Shall We?

Whether you have been working for 20 years or 20 days, it is human nature to focus on the most recent job. Even if it boasted the shortest tenure. Even if a previous job was for years and the current one just for months. Why? Because the interviewer wants to know what you can do for him or her—right now—and the most current job offers the best available proof.

 Why are you thinking of leaving your current job?

What do they want to hear?

Obviously, no one wants to leave a job with which they are completely content (although some people routinely interview to keep "in practice" or stay in touch with what is currently on offer). But the last thing you want to do is appear negative or, worse, speak badly about your current employer. (Your interviewer will assume, fair or not, that, if hired, you will soon be characterizing his or her company in the same disparaging terms.)

So handle your discontent (if that's what led you here) very gingerly. The less contented you are, the more careful you should be in talking about it. It will do you absolutely no good to confess to the interviewer that you lie awake nights fantasizing about putting a contract out on your current boss.

Instead, do some of what management consultants call "visioning." Imagine the ideal next step in your career. Then act as though you are interviewing for that position.

Here's what I mean. Let's say you are interested in assuming more financial management responsibilities. You might tell the interviewer:

> *"There is a great deal I enjoy about my current job. But my potential for growth in this area is limited at Closely Held, Inc., because of the size of the company and the fact that expansion is not a part of its current strategic plan."*

Green light

Unless you have been fired or laid off, you should make it clear that you are sitting in front of the interviewer only because you seek more responsibility, a bigger challenge, better opportunities for growth—even more money—*not* because you are desperate to put some distance between yourself and your current job situation.

Emphasize your desire to move "up" rather than just to move "out."

Avoid any personal and/or negative comments about co-workers, supervisors, or your current (last) company's policies.

Red light

The introduction of any negative, no matter how horrible your current job situation. (In fact, the more obviously horrible your job, the more points you will score with many interviewers for creating an impression of relative contentment.)

A willingness to make a lateral move or even take a demotion just to leave your current company. Unless you are moving into an entirely new area or field, such a willingness to move "out" rather than "up" would give *me* pause. What are you hiding? Is this just a last-ditch effort to get out before you are shoved out? And what does such a willingness say about your ability to "tough it out" until the right situation comes along? Is my company just a calmer sea in which to tread water until the right freighter passes by?

A candidate who admits she lies awake nights fantasizing about calling Joe "No Knees" Buzzano to "discipline" her current boss.

Variation

➲ *What's hindering your progress at your present firm?*

Q: Where does your boss think you are now?

What do they want to hear?

Although you may have been given notice or laid off and, therefore, be interviewing with the full knowledge of your boss, it's more likely you're still employed. So under no circumstances mutter something like, "He thinks I'm interviewing with you so I can leave that hellhole behind. By the way, he'll be calling you tomorrow to find a job himself." You should attempt to schedule interviews during lunch hour, after work, or on a personal or vacation day. I personally don't like to hear that a candidate has taken a sick day to talk with me. It's a "white" lie but a lie nevertheless.

Green light

The truth, whatever it is. Many interviewers will give you points for demonstrating your sense of responsibility to your current job by scheduling a breakfast interview or one during a lunch hour or after hours.

Red light

If you have blatantly lied or indicate through body language that the question makes you uncomfortable (implying that you lied).

If your answer demonstrates little or no loyalty to the company that's still paying the bills, whether that organization is enlightened or despotic.

Q: Are you still employed at the last firm listed on your resume?

What do they want to hear?

You probably know the adage that it's always easier to find a job when you already have one. Well, it's true, because many interviewers, fair or not, believe that an employed person is somehow "better" than an unemployed one, even if the latter is more qualified. Being laid off is perceived by many interviewers as a sign of weakness. I even heard one experienced executive recruiter say, "Oh, if she was laid off, there must be something wrong with her. Companies don't ever let really good employees go!" Would that it were true!

But the fact is that massive layoffs, while not as frequent or disruptive as a few years ago, can and do still occur. And many hard-working, loyal individuals who contributed greatly to their companies—and could be significant assets to a new one—have to admit they've been laid off. Personally, I am firmly convinced that there is no shame in this status and give a laid-off candidate the same consideration I do anyone else. I would not assume all interviewers are as enlightened.

And if you were fired? Come clean quickly and smoothly to turn this potential negative into a positive.

Let's consider the case of Nick. A hotel sales manager, he was unfortunate enough to work for a petty tyrant who made a practice of taking Nick and his co-workers to task often, publicly and mercilessly.

One day, Nick finally had it. He blew up at his boss—and was fired on the spot. Later on, he was asked about his employment status in an interview for another hotel sales job. He answered bluntly, "I was fired."

When the stunned interviewer asked to hear more, Nick explained:

> *"My boss and I just didn't get along, and I have to admit I didn't handle the situation well. I certainly understand the importance of call reports and log sheets and other sales-management controls. I guess I interpreted some of Joe's quick demands for these things as a lack of trust, and I shouldn't have. I've learned my lesson."*

Green light

Talk less about why you were terminated and more about what you've learned from the experience.

If you were laid off, or, as the British quaintly say, "made redundant," you shouldn't be expected to apologize. You might say something like, "Yes, I was one of 16 people laid off when sales took a slide." (This is an easy way out—presuming you were not a member of the sales department!)

Red light

As always, the introduction of any negative. ("Yeah, I was fired because I'm not as young as I used to be. Wait until they see what my old lawyer has to say about age discrimination. I'll make them pay through the nose!")

Being fired for cause, especially if you refuse to admit responsibility or to detail what steps have been taken to correct the problem. Celebrity felons like Mike Tyson may get two or three or umpteen chances to make millions even after serving time, but most interviewers get a bit antsy about hiring someone who was fired for stealing, drinking on the job, hitting their boss, or some equally charming offense.

Let's play "gotcha"

Q: Describe the way your department is organized. Also, what is the title of the person to whom you report? What are his or her exact responsibilities?

What do they want to hear?

Did you hear that? If you've been vastly exaggerating the duties and responsibilities of your current position, that sound you heard was the door that just closed...behind you...on your way out of the interview.

This question is designed to clarify what you really do— how can you be doing "X" if you said that's your *boss's* main function?—and set up a series of follow-up questions about why you exaggerated (presuming the interviewer doesn't just say "thank you" then and there).

Green light

Duties and responsibilities that match those claimed on your resume.

Duties and responsibilities commensurate with the job at hand.

An answer that ties in with your answers to previous questions about work experience. The more detailed these answers, the easier it will be for an interviewer to catch any inconsistencies (at which point he or she will return to those previous answers and ask why the current one doesn't seem to mesh with them).

A clearly presented explanation of how your department, division, or company is set up, which tends to at least show consistency with your resume and implies that you have really done what you said you have (although a really good interviewer will take detailed notes so he can check each particular with your supervisor when he calls for a reference).

Red light

A hazy, vague explanation that indicates you may be making it all up as you go along.

Glaring inconsistencies with your resume or previous answers.

Failure to include a key responsibility or job duty that was previously proclaimed, especially if it's one that is important to the new job.

An organizational plan that doesn't make sense to the interviewer. (The more experience you have at different companies, the more likely you will have been exposed to different structures and management styles, and the more confident you will feel that a structure that seems top heavy or one that gives lower-level staff members an extraordinary amount of freedom doesn't "feel right.")

Columbo is on the warpath

Q: Tell me about your typical day at your current (last) job. How much time do you spend on the phone? In meetings? In one-on-one chats? Working by yourself? Working with your team (or others)?

What do they want to hear?

Again, they are looking for the detail that will "prove" some of the earlier general statements you made (about responsibilities, duties, even favorite aspects of your job) or show that those statements were disingenuous or perhaps somewhat excessive.

Variations

➲ *On a typical day, tell me what you do in the first and last hour at work. When do you arrive and leave?*

➲ *Tell me what specific responsibilities you currently delegate. Are you delegating too many or too few tasks? Why? What's stopping you from changing it?*

➲ *How many hours per week do you have to work to fulfill your responsibilities at work?*

➲ *What's the most important part of your current job to you? To your firm?*

  How long have you been looking for a job?

What do they want to hear?

Unless you've been fired or laid off, your answer should always be that you've just started looking. If you think the interviewer has some way of finding out that you've been looking for a while (perhaps you've come to him through a recruiter who knows your history), be prepared to explain why you haven't received or accepted any offers.

Rightly or wrongly, many interviewers presume that the longer you've been out there, the less desirable you are to hire. Personally, I disagree. If someone's been looking for a month or two or three, are they inherently less desirable than a newly minted *ex*-employee who's still wearing his company T-shirt under his suit? Given the near-full employment in the United States right now, it's unrealistic to expect that everyone who wants a job can find one right away. It's even less realistic not to assume that the most qualified candidates might well be picky and simply be ensuring a proper "fit" with the right company before plunging back into the corporate seas.

Nevertheless, be prepared to deal with those interviewers less understanding than I.

 ## Why haven't you received any offers so far?

What do they want to hear?

You're just as choosy about finding the right job as the interviewer is about hiring the right candidate. Don't whine or show that the search is upsetting you. If you've already fielded an offer or two, you might say:

> *"I have had an offer. But the situation was not right for me. I'm especially glad that I didn't accept, because I now have a shot at landing this position."*

It's important to tell the truth, however, because the interviewer's next logical question may be the following:

 ## Who made you an offer? For what type of position? At what salary?

What do they want to hear?

If you've already lied, you're in hot water now! Some interviewers will consider any admission of lying in these circumstances your "voluntary" offer to end the interview!

Many interviewers know a great deal about their competitors and which positions they're trying to fill. If you did the smart thing and told the truth, give the interviewer the name of the company.

It's important to stress that the position you turned down was very similar to the one you're applying for now. After all, if the job you are currently interviewing for is perfect for you—as you've undoubtedly already told the interviewer three or four times—why would you be at all interested in something very different at the other company?

 If you don't leave your current job, what will happen there? How far do you expect to advance?

What do they want to hear?

Is desperation driving you away from your current job, so that you'll say or do anything to get this one? This doesn't exactly make you a prime candidate to most interviewers. Why should he or she save you?

Remember the adage: "There's no better time to look for a new job than when you're happy with your old job." Even if you'd rather hawk peanuts at the stadium than stay another month at ABC Widget, convince the interviewer that you're the type of employee who is capable of making the most of any situation—even an employment situation you've just said you want to leave.

You could say:

"Naturally I'm interested in this job and have been thinking about leaving ABC. However, my supervisors think highly of me, and I expect that one day other

situations will open up for me at the company. I'm one of ABC's top salespeople. I have seen other people performing at similar levels advance to management positions. That's what I'm looking for right now."

Whatever your feeling about your current job, it's always best to conduct your part of the interview as if you are in the driver's seat, just cruising along happily until you see that changing lanes would improve your career. You certainly aren't interested in getting off at the next exit, no matter where it leads!

Begin your answers with the phrase, "Well, assuming I'm not the successful candidate for this position...." Without too much ego, let the interviewer know that you're taking your time. You're interested in choosing a job that's right for you.

Green light

If you can claim (or do claim) that you will still advance and be given more responsibility, but perhaps at too slow a pace or without adequate compensation.

If you are able to describe a situation in which the company, through little or no fault of yours, will clearly not be able to keep or pay its top people what they're worth (for example: a pending merger, bankruptcy, cash flow problems, loss of a key customer or product). Clearly, your reason for leaving is obvious and justifiable and your future there dim, through no fault of your own.

Red light

"Well, I doubt I'll last the week. Old Scrawnynose will probably fire me right after lunch."

An answer that indicates problems at the company for which you must bear some responsibility. ("Well, sales are down 10 percent across the board but my territory is down 72 percent. It's not *my* fault that all those stores went out of business!")

Well, er, uh, I ...

Although it's a good idea to convince your prospective employer that the world is your oyster—and you're simply waiting to find the perfect pearl of a job—you might get hit with questions like these:

 If you're so happy at your current job, why are you leaving? Will they be surprised?

What do they want to hear?

You might think your current company will go out of business at any second. Or you may be leaving because you just broke off your engagement with the person in the office next door. Don't cry on the interviewer's shoulder.

Instead, reassure him or her that you're not running away from anything. You've made the decision to move toward:

- ➲ More responsibility.
- ➲ More knowledge.
- ➲ The wonderful opportunity available at Good Times, Inc.

Variations

- ➲ *What would have to change at your current job to make it tenable?*

⊃ *What have you had to change about yourself/your skills/your philosophy/your duties to adapt to changes at your current firm?*

 If you have these complaints about your current job/boss/company, and they think so highly of you, why haven't you brought your concerns to their attention?

What do they want to hear?

The interviewer is trying to "hoist you by your own petard." Some problem-solver you are! You can't even talk to your boss about changes that might make you happier!

If you do find yourself cornered, facing this dead end, the only way out is to be as positive as possible. Say something like:

"Grin & Bear It is aware of my desire to move up. But the company is still small. There's really not much they can do about it. The management team is terrific. There's no need right now to add to it, and they are aware of some of the problems this creates in keeping good performers. It's something they talk about quite openly."

Variations

⊃ *If you could eliminate one duty/ responsibility from your current (last) job, what would it be and why?*

> ➲ *If you could make one comment or suggestion to your current boss, what would it be? Did you do anything of the sort? Why or why not?*

Oh, you got to have friends

 ## How would your co-workers describe you?

What do they want to hear?

Of course, they would describe you as an easy going person who is a good team player. After all, you've found that "a lot more can be accomplished when people gang up on a problem, rather than on each other."

Once again, the personal inventory you completed in Chapter 1 will come in handy. Cull words from the lists you've titled "My strongest skills," "My greatest areas of knowledge," "My greatest personality strengths," and "The things I do best"—and put them in the mouths of co-workers and friends.

Variations

> ➲ *What five adjectives would your last supervisor use to describe you?*

> ➲ *How effectively did your supervisor conduct appraisals?*

> ➲ *How did you do on your last performance appraisal?*

⮞   *What were your key strengths and weaknesses mentioned by your supervisor?*

⮞   *How did your last supervisor get the best performance out of you?*

⮞   *What did you say and do the last time you were right and your boss was* wrong?

Haven't we been here before?

 Give me specific examples of what you did at your current (last) job to increase revenues, reduce costs, be more efficient, save effort, etc.

What do they want to hear?

This ties in to the earlier questions you were asked about budgetary responsibility and how your current department is organized. (Savvy interviewers think it's a good idea after asking the first question or two to ask some different questions, *then* return to the subject later. Many candidates, having successfully navigated the shoals of the earlier questions, may be caught in an exaggeration when the interviewer returns to the question later on rather than following it up immediately.)

I'd like 10 weeks' vacation, sir!

 What do you feel an employer owes an employee?

What do they want to hear?

This is not—let me repeat, *not*—your invitation to discuss the employee benefits package you would like to have. It's a loaded question.

Don't get into a dissertation on the employer's moral responsibility to employees. For that matter, don't get into legal responsibilities. Try to refocus the interviewer's attention on your positive outlook, and keep your answer short and sweet.

> *"I think an employer owes its employees opportunity. In my next position, I look forward to the opportunity to run projects profitably."*

If the interviewer digs for a more specific response about a sensitive issue—such as your feelings about the information an employer should share with employees, or the size of the raise pool—you could respond like this:

> *"I hope that my employer will be respectful of me as an employee and of any agreements we may negotiate in the course of business. However, I know that there are times when organizations face tough decisions that may require confidentiality and affect employees. That's business."*

What if pigs could fly and...

Hypothetical ("what if...?") questions are the basis of a situational interview, in which the interviewer conjures up a series of situations, real or imaginary, in order to ascertain whether you have the resourcefulness, logic, creativity, and ability to think under pressure. Why apply such pressure? Even the best-prepared candidates can't prepare for *these* questions!

Situational interview questions can come in any shape or style. I've given you only a handful of samples here. But once you get the idea, see if you can outsmart the interviewer. If you have a detailed description of the job you're applying for, use your imagination to try to anticipate a number of situations that might come up once you're behind the desk.

Q: Your supervisor left an assignment in your in-box, then left for the week. You can't reach him and you don't fully understand the assignment. What would you do? What do they want to hear?

The interviewer is attempting to gauge whether you have an appropriate respect for hierarchy and deadline demands. Alternatively, it may be a way for a more entrepreneurial firm to see whether you are willing to make decisions when forced to, even if, inevitably, mistakes will occur.

If there is truly no way to reach your boss or leave a message via voice mail or e- mail, you'd suck up the courage to approach your boss' supervisor.

Of course, you would do this in a way that would not reflect badly on your boss by explaining that you and your boss simply missed the chance to discuss the assignment before he had to leave the office. Because you're not yet familiar with the company's procedures, you simply want to be sure that you understand the assignment, so you can start on it as soon as possible.

Q: The successful candidate for this position will be working with some highly trained individuals who have been with the company for a long time. How will you mesh with them?

What do they want to hear?

Your answer should indicate your eagerness—as the new kid on the block—to learn from your future co-workers. You don't want to raise any doubts about how they might react to you. So convey the fact that, while you are certainly bringing something to the party (skills, knowledge, your own insights), you realize you have a lot to learn from the people you'll be working with (even if, in your heart of hearts, you think they're probably a bunch of old fogies and can't wait to get on board and shape them up).

 Your supervisor tells you to do something in a way you know is dead wrong. What do you do?

What do they want to hear?

This is a tough question, so why not acknowledge it with an answer like this:

> *"In a situation like this, even the best employee runs the risk of seeming insubordinate. I would pose my alternative to my supervisor in the most deferential way possible. If he insisted that I was wrong, I guess I'd have to do it his way."*

 If you were unfairly criticized by your supervisor, what would you do?

What do they want to hear?

All of us can think back to a time when the pressure was on at work and a mistake was made. Maybe you took more than your fair share of the blame. Perhaps you were caught in circumstances beyond your control. In any event, your boss blamed you. But chances are, you and your boss got through the rough spot and you made sure the mistake never occurred again.

You could answer the question by telling of such an experience. You do not have to select the most vulnerable or perilous moment of your career to illustrate the point. Simple mistakes are more than adequate:

> *"In the course of my career there have been a few times when problems have come up and I have been held accountable for mistakes I did not feel I had caused. But a problem is a problem no matter who creates it, and you certainly don't have to create the problem to solve it. The most important thing is to deal with it.*
>
> *"On those occasions when the issue has been significant enough, I have explained my point of view to my supervisor later—after the situation has been resolved and the atmosphere has calmed."*

 ## Would you like to have your boss's job? Why or why not?

What do they want to hear?

No matter how you answer this question, the interviewer will learn a lot about you, so proceed with caution. It's an indirect way of finding out whether or not you want to be promoted.

Let's start with the first part of the question: Saying yes indicates you're ambitious and interested in career advancement. Saying no indicates doubts or reservations, at least about the job in question.

In the second part of the question, things get sticky. For instance, if it's clear that you're interested in promotion and the position you are applying for doesn't offer a direct path to a higher level, then the interviewer may conclude that you'll be disappointed. On the other hand, in a highly competitive organization, expressing reservations about career advancement could knock you out of the running immediately.

There are two things you should do to prepare for this question. First, in your preliminary research, get a sense of the corporate culture and opportunities for advancement. Try to be aware of the possibilities going into the interview.

Second, know what your honest answer to the question is. Maybe you're ready, willing, and anxious to move up and take on your boss's job. Or maybe you shudder at the thought of a management job where you have to deal with personnel issues. "Know thyself" on this one, because if you're hired, your answer can come back to haunt you.

Now put the results together to develop your response. Ideally, your honest answer will suit the company. If your aspirations are incompatible with the possibilities, you can—at your own risk—compensate by offering an answer that fits. No matter what, make it *positive*.

> *"In time, I would love to have my boss's job. I'm particularly interested in the vendor relationships and sales promotion sides of buying."*

> *"I am very interested in career advancement, but my current boss's responsibilities are heavily weighted toward managing department production. In time, I hope to move into a position with primary responsibility for design quality."*

> *"I would be open to taking on additional responsibilities, but I like the autonomy of a sales position, and I find it rewarding to work directly with clients. My boss is mainly responsible for supervising the department and its personnel. In such a position, I would miss the client contact."*

How to shine in any situational interview

➲ **Admit that a tough situation would make you nervous.** You might even panic momentarily. No interviewer is looking for a candidate bent on plunging right in—and then flailing about without thinking of consequences or alternatives. Nervousness calls forth the adrenaline that often fuels creative strategies.

➲ **Take a moment to think before you answer.** This shows you are not likely to plunge into any situation with a hotheaded response. Rather, you are taking time to weigh the alternatives and choose the best course of action.

➲ **Avoid throwing the "bull."** No matter what the interview technique, quash the temptation to exaggerate or downright fabricate a response.

➲ **Show that you have a grasp of the real world.** Admit that you have a lot to learn about this company and the position. This approach is far more effective than trying to sell yourself as a savior.

➲ **Plan your answers to a number of different situations ahead of time.** Assume that some of these questions will be about areas of knowledge and skill you have yet to develop, so learn as much as you can about what you don't know. And have a strategy for finding the information or resources you currently lack.

Chapter Eight

So Why Us?

In most prizefights, the first couple of rounds are relatively boring. The boxers spend their time checking each other out—testing each other's feints and jabs—before the serious pummeling begins.

The same could be said of most interviews. After the first bell, the pleasantries begin. The second bell signals the "getting-to-know-you" round of questioning. Then, if the interviewer thinks it's worthwhile, he begins "pummeling" you—with questions meant to separate the "stiffs" from the real contenders.

If you've already confidently answered a dozen or so questions, you're in that "pummeling" stage. Your chance to dance around open-ended questions is long gone. In order to make it to the final bell, you need to demonstrate some real knowledge.

 Do you know much about our company?

What do they want to hear?

Believe it or not, many candidates think this is merely an icebreaker and simply answer, "No."

Don't *you* follow suit! After all, why would you go into one of the most important encounters of your life so thoroughly unprepared? And then *admit* it?

I have urged (okay, nagged) you to do your homework. This is where your research will come in handy. Toss out a few salient (and positive) facts about the company, and finish by lobbing a question that demonstrates your interest back into the interviewer's court. For example:

> *"Boy, what a growth story Starter Up is! Didn't I read recently that you've had seven straight years of double-digit growth? I read in your annual report that you're planning to introduce a new line of products in the near future. I jumped at the chance to apply here. Can you tell me a little bit about this division and the position you're interviewing for?"*

Green light

Any answer that demonstrates your pre-interview research. The more informed you are, the more likely you should end up at the top of the list of potential employees.

A detailed answer that indicates the breadth of your research, from checking out the company's Internet site, to reading its annual report and being familiar with its products and services. Referring to a trade magazine article that mentions the company or, better yet, *the interviewer*, is a nice touch, don't you think?

Company research for $100, Alex

 Do you have any questions?

What do they want to hear?

Normally, this question occurs very near the end of the interview. In fact, you may well assume that its appearance pretty much signals the end. Nevertheless, because we've been talking about the importance of your pre-interview research, this is as good a place as any to address this question.

Never, I repeat, *never* answer with a no. How can you make one of the most important decisions of your life—whether to work for this company at this job—without knowing more?

Even if you think you're sold on the position or you're clear on the responsibilities, you must speak up here. If you don't, the interviewer will assume you are uninterested. And that can be the kiss of death to you as an applicant, even at this late stage.

What do *you* want to know?

It's easy to get caught up in the challenge of impressing the interviewer with your brilliant answers, but it's also important that you don't lose sight of the fact that you have a goal—trying to determine whether this situation is right for you, whether this job is worthy of your talents and commitment.

With this in mind, here are a few key questions *I* would want to ask:

> *"Can you give me a formal, written description of the position? I'm interested in reviewing in detail the major activities involved and what results are expected."*

This is a good question to pose to the screening interviewer. It will help you prepare to face the hiring manager. If a written description doesn't exist, ask the interviewer to dictate as complete a description of the job to you as possible.

> *"Does this job usually lead to other positions at the company? Which ones?"*

You don't want to find yourself in a dead-end job. So find out how you can expect to advance after you land this job. What happened to the person you would be replacing? Is he or she still with the company? If so, doing what?

Try to pursue this line of questioning without giving the impression that you can't wait to get *out* of a job you don't even *have* yet! If you ask in a completely nonthreatening manner, your ambition will be understood—and even welcomed.

> *"Tell me some of the particular skills or attributes that you want in the candidate for this position?"*

The interviewer's answer should tell you how much your traits are valued. With this information, you can underline those traits you possess at the close of the interview to end it on a strong note.

> *"Please tell me a little bit about the people with whom I'll be working most closely."*

I wish someone had told me about this question before my last job interview! The answer can tell you so many things. For example: How good the people you are working with are at their jobs and how much you are likely to learn from them. Most important, you'll find out whether the hiring manager seems enthusiastic about his or her team.

A hiring manager usually tries to put on his or her best face during an interview, just as you do as the prospective candidate. But catching the interviewer off guard with this question can give you a glimpse of the real feelings hiding behind the "game face."

If he or she doesn't seem enthusiastic, you probably won't enjoy being part of the team. This particular hiring manager may attribute little success, and perhaps a lot of headaches, to the people who work for him or her.

"What do you like best about this company? Why?"

If the interviewer hems and haws a lot over this one, it may indicate that she doesn't really like the company that much at all.

If she's instantly enthusiastic, her answer should help sell you on her and the company.

The answer to this question can also give you a good sense of the values of the organization and the hiring manager. If she talks about nothing but products and how well her stock options are doing, it indicates a lack of enthusiasm for the people-side of the business.

"What is the company's ranking within the industry? Does this position represent a change from where it was a few years ago?"

You should already have some indication of the answer to this question from your initial research, particularly if the company is publicly owned. If you have some of this information, go ahead and build it into your question:

"I've read that the company has risen from fifth to second in market share in just the past three years. What are the key reasons for this dramatic success?"

Do shy away from asking about days off, vacation, holidays, sick pay, personal days, and so on. You'll seem like someone who is looking for a chance to get out of the office before you even start!

Here's the most comprehensive list of questions I can devise. Again, attempt to gain answers to them *before* the interview (although this will not always be possible, especially if you are interviewing with a small, privately held company).

Questions about the company

- ⟳ What are the company's leading products or services? What products or services is it planning to introduce in the near future?
- ⟳ What are the company's key markets and are those markets growing?
- ⟳ Will the company be entering any new markets in the next couple of years? Which ones and via what kind of distribution channel(s)?
- ⟳ What growth rate are you currently anticipating? Will this be accomplished internally or through acquisitions?
- ⟳ Who owns the company?
- ⟳ Please tell me about your own tenure with the XYZ Company.
- ⟳ How many employees work for the organization? In how many offices? In this office?
- ⟳ Is the company planning to grow through acquisitions?

➲ What has been the company's layoff history in the last five years? Do you anticipate any cutbacks in the near future and, if you do, how will they impact my department or position?

➲ What major problems or challenges has the company recently faced? How were they addressed? What results do you expect?

➲ What is the company's share of each of its markets?

➲ Which other companies serving those markets pose a serious threat?

➲ Please tell me more about your training programs. Do you offer reimbursement for job-related education? Time off?

➲ What is your hiring philosophy?

➲ What are the company's plans and prospects for growth and expansion?

➲ What are the company's goals in the next few years?

➲ What do *you* like best about this company? Why?

➲ What is the company's ranking within the industry? Does this represent a change from where it was a year or a few years ago?

Questions about the department or division

➲ Explain the organizational structure of the department and its primary functions and responsibilities.

➲ To whom will I be reporting? To whom does he or she report?

➲ With which other departments does this department work most closely?

- How many people work exclusively in this department?
- What problems is this department facing? What are its current goals and objectives?

Questions about the job

- What kind of training should I expect and for how long?
- How many people will be reporting to me?
- Is relocation an option, a possibility, or a requirement?
- How did this job become available? Was the previous person promoted? What is their new title? Was the previous person fired? Why?
- Would I be able to speak with the person who held this job previously?
- Is a written job description available?
- Could you describe a typical day in this position?
- How long has this position been available?
- How many other candidates have you interviewed? How many more candidates will you be interviewing before you make a decision?
- Is there no one from within the organization who is qualified for this position?
- Before you're able to reach a hiring decision, how many more interviews should I expect to go through and with whom?
- Where will I be working? May I see my office/cubicle/closet/floormat?
- How advanced/current is the hardware and software I will be expected to use?
- How much day-to-day autonomy will I have?

⟳ Does this job usually lead to other positions in the company? Which ones?

⟳ Please tell me a little bit about the people with whom I'll be working most closely.

It's the interviewer's turn again

Q: **What interests you most about this position? Our company?**

What do they want to hear?

You know the drill from some of the previous chapters. You have your eye on more responsibility, more opportunities, the chance to supervise more people, and the chance to develop a new set of skills and sharpen the ones you've already acquired. And, of course, if they absolutely *insist* they'll increase your salary, well, you certainly aren't one to be negative and say no!

However, this is also the ideal time to show what you know about this company and how the position you're interviewing for can contribute to its success.

 Green light

Armed with this knowledge, you might reply: "I've heard so much about your titanium ball bearings that I've wanted to experiment with different applications for them." Rather than, "I'll have a better commute if I get this job." (Unbelievably, I have heard this response from more than one candidate I've interviewed! It may be honest—even important to the candidate— but it sure wasn't the answer *I* wanted to hear!)

Red light

Be careful of any answer that clearly demonstrates incompatibility—if your primary interest lies in an area that will be peripheral, at best, to your real function, you're just setting yourself up for a "thank you, we'll be in touch."

Variation

⤷ *On a scale of one to five, rate your interest in this company. In this job.*

From Jekyll to Hyde

Q: **What have you heard about our company that you *don't* like?**

What do they want to hear?

This is tricky. Obviously you want to minimize the negative implications of any question, including this one. If there hasn't been any dire news, you could ask about the dearth of the most recent software or your wish that the company's profits were a bit more predictable.

Of course, the existence of real news changes your response. Maybe you've heard that ABC Widget had a layoff 12 months ago and you're wondering if the dust has settled yet. Or perhaps you've heard rumors of a merger.

Don't play dumb. Given either of the above scenarios, any new prospect would have reservations about the company's stability and plans for the future. If the interviewer opens the door for you to ask what might otherwise be uncomfortable questions, by all means walk right in.

Just don't slam it in your own face by raising a huge negative: "I'm not sure I like the fact that I'll be reporting to three different executives" or "Is it possible to be scheduled for a salary review in 30 days?"

This is a much larger (smaller) company than you've worked for. How do you feel about that?

What do they want to hear?

If the company is larger, you are undoubtedly looking forward to terrific growth opportunities and exposure to more areas of knowledge than you have access to now.

If the prospective company is smaller, you are looking forward to a far less bureaucratic organization, where decisions can be made much more quickly and where no department is so large that it is not extremely familiar with the workings of the entire company.

What are you looking for in your next job?

What do they want to hear?

Obviously, you should tailor your response to the job you're applying for. But answering with a slightly reorganized rendition of the job description isn't the right way to go about it.

Interviewers typically ask a question like this to gauge your level of interest in the job and see if you have any doubts. So focus on the job at hand. Think of key skills the job requires and emphasize your interest in having a chance to develop (or *further* develop) one of them. And don't forget to express enthusiasm for your field of work. Here is an example:

"In my current position as development research associate, I research corporate and government funding opportunities and write grant proposals. I enjoy my work very much, but my contact with prospective donors has been limited. I look forward to a position that offers more opportunities to work with donors, securing their support, and insuring that they are recognized for their contributions.

"I have had a few opportunities to do this with my current employer, and based on my success in dealing with Timely Donations, Inc., I know I can successfully advocate an organization's mission to gain needed corporate support."

 What aspect of the job I've described appeals to you least?

What do they want to hear?

Let me lead with a little humor. After conversing with his Irish friend one day, a man finally blurted out in consternation, "Why do the Irish always answer a question with a question?" Unruffled, the Irishman winked and replied, "Do we now?"

Your best tactic is to follow suit. Shoot the question right back at the interviewer! For example, you might say:

"You've described a position in which I'd be over-seeing some extraordinary levels of output. What sort of quality-control procedures does this company have? Will I be able to consult with in-house specialists?"

Much like the question asked earlier ("What have you heard about our company that you don't like?"), I would presume this question is inviting a real answer. If you aren't going to take the

job (unbeknownst to the interviewer) because of what you believe to be a fundamental flaw in the job or the company, a good
interviewer will want to know about it.

One of three possible scenarios will result:

❶ You'll reveal an objection that isn't valid. Once the
interviewer answers it, you will again be an
interested candidate.

❷ You'll reveal a viable objection that leads the
interviewer to eliminate you from consideration.

❸ You'll reveal a viable objection that will lead you to
remove *yourself* from consideration.

  **Based on what you know about
our industry, how does your ideal
job stack up against the description
of the job for which you're applying?**

What do they want to hear?

The "ideal" job is always one in which you'll have a broad
scope of responsibilities that will enable you to continue to learn
about your industry and grow. So use your knowledge about the
industry to formulate a reply that, though perhaps a bit idealis-
tic, doesn't sound unrealistic:

> *"I know that many accounting firms are deriving
> more and more of their fee income from consulting ser-
> vices. I'd like a job that combines my cost-accounting
> knowledge with client consultation and problem solv-
> ing. Ideally, I'd like to start as part of a team, then
> eventually head up a practice in a specific area, say,
> cost accounting in manufacturing environments."*

Now, based on what you know about the position, touch on one (and only one) minor shortcoming, and formulate a few careful questions about some aspects of the position you don't know about. Expanding on the above example, you might say:

> *"I know this position is in the auditing area and that you hire many of your entry-level people into that department. I must confess, I would like this to be a stepping stone to working more in the manufacturing area and, several years down the line, in consulting. I'm sure I don't have the requisite knowledge or experience yet. Is this a position in which I can gain such experience, and is this a career track that's possible at this firm?"*

Q: How will you handle the least interesting or most unpleasant parts of this job?

What do they want to hear?

An interviewer posing this question usually will build in specific aspects of the position, such as: "You won't always be looking for creative solutions to our clients' tax problems. Most of the time, you'll be churning out returns and making sure you comply with the latest laws. You're aware of that, of course?" You might answer:

> *"I'm sure that every job in the accounting field has its routine tasks. They have to be done, too. Doing those tasks is part of the satisfaction of doing the job well. They make the relatively infrequent chances we have to be creative even more satisfying."*

You've had little experience with budgeting (or sales or whatever). How do you intend to learn what you need to know to perform on this job?

What do they want to hear?

"Well, throughout my career, I've proven to be a quick study. For example, when my company's inventory system was computerized, I didn't have the time to go through the training. But the company that supplied the software had developed some computer-based tutorials and training manuals. I studied them and practiced at home. I hope that I'd be able to do something similar to pick up the rudiments of your budgeting system."

You could also mention other options, such as learning from professional publications and seminars. Show your initiative and resourcefulness in getting up to speed quickly. The interviewer wants to be sure you won't just be sitting around twiddling your thumbs and complaining that you don't know what to do next. Reassure him or her that you plan to do whatever it takes to go right on learning throughout your tenure.

Now, how would you step in and save the day? If you don't know as much as you'd like to about the position for which you're interviewing, spend some time with industry and trade publications. Focus on articles written to help people in this type of position solve common problems—or that suggest tips, tricks, and tools designed to increase everyday efficiency.

You want to demonstrate that you're ready to step right in and handle a tough situation with a cool head.

It's also a good idea to sharpen your working knowledge and skills. Interviewers like to pose problems you can solve on the spot. These exercises are intended to demonstrate your proficiency in the areas most important to the job.

Preparation makes perfect. If you come up blank, or use a fact or formula inaccurately during one of these exercises, it will be difficult, if not impossible, to recoup your credibility. That would be especially unfortunate after you've gotten this far.

Caveat: Different companies may use slightly different terms for the same procedure or material. So explain your terminology up front to make sure you're communicating clearly.

 How long do you plan to stay with us?

What do they want to hear?

One answer I *don't* want to hear is "forever," because I simply won't believe it (and I'll wonder about the intelligence of a candidate who would think that's what I want to hear). You should offer a fairly simple answer along the lines of "as long as I continue to grow, continue to learn, and continue to contribute in ways you feel are valuable."

I'm not sure whether this question will ever give an interviewer any useful information, because any candidate candid (or stupid) enough to answer "oh, a month or two, until I find a job I really like" shouldn't have made it through the screening process (or, for that matter, the first 10 questions of the interview). But be careful your body language doesn't reveal your real answer. Squirming *does* seem to mean "oh, a month or two, until I find a job I really like!"

If you already appear to be a job-hopper but trot out the standard "as long as I continue to grow, etc." speech, don't be surprised if the interviewer asks, "Is that what you told the interviewers at your four previous positions?" Whatever you do, don't answer, "Yep, and they all believed me, too!"

How do you think I've handled this interview?

What do they want to hear?

Well, now, your options aren't very pleasant, are they? Saying "lousy" doesn't seem appropriate, but "great, sir, and may I polish your shoes?" seems a bit too obsequious. There is no right answer, much like the hypothetical questions in a situational interview, so don't offer one—ask a question of your own instead.

Let's get personal

Most people think that the candidate who talks only about work, work, work stands the best chance of getting the job. But there's a "you" that exists after 5 p.m.—and most interviewers want to get to know that person, too.

The guiding principle for answering personal questions is the same as it is for responding to queries about your professional experiences: Emphasize the positive. Let the interviewer in on the best and most interesting aspects of your personality.

The double-edged sword

Just be careful of saying too much. Your answers can reveal more information than the interviewer is entitled by law to ask for. For example, in the warm glow of an interview that seems to be going well, you might feel comfortable talking about your children—and the challenges of being a single parent.

The interviewer could *not* have asked about your family situation in order to eliminate you from the running. Yet once this information is out, it's fair game. He or she is free to use it to make unfair judgments about your ability to handle various aspects of the job. If the job you're applying for involves occasional overnight travel, for example, he or she may decide your family situation would create unnecessary difficulties.

So, while these questions do give you an opportunity to demonstrate what a terrific person you are, they could also prompt you to—unwittingly—provide information that does you in as a prospective candidate for employment! Make sure to study Chapter 9 to identify questions that are, at best, inappropriate and, at worst, illegal.

To your good health

Employers have more than just a passing interest in your health. Most companies are looking for ways to keep the overall cost of health care insurance from skyrocketing. Most managers want to know that you won't be felled by every flu bug that makes the rounds—and on sick leave when they need you most.

 ### Are you in good health? What do you do to stay in shape?

You must be honest in answering this one. Prospective employers can find ways to check your medical history if they're worried about your health. In fact, many employers make job offers contingent on your passing a physical examination.

If you appear to be dedicated to maintaining your own good health, you'll ease many of their concerns. You don't have to be an exercise nut. Just play up any activities you do regularly that provide at least some health benefit, such as yard work, home repairs, even walking the dog.

Do you have any physical problems that may limit your ability to perform this job?

This is a perfectly legitimate question for the interviewer to ask. So be honest. Are you applying for a job that requires a lot of data entry despite the fact that you've been waging an ongoing battle with carpal tunnel syndrome? Will you be doing a lot more walking and standing on the job that might trigger that problem knee?

Remember, though, the key words are "ability to perform this job." A physical problem that is *not* job-related is *not* pertinent...and none of the employer's business, by law.

 How do you manage to balance career and family?

What do they want to hear?

Gosh, you are facing one tricky devil. Again, this is a perfectly legal question, but it does make it decidedly difficult if you are determined to keep any discussion of family out of the interview. Why would you want to avoid such a discussion? If you've been around the block a few times, you may legitimately worry that the interviewer has some unwritten rules, such as no single parents hired for travel positions (or, for that matter, no parents if travel exceeds X percent).

Accordingly, if you're attempting to give an answer that is as unrevealing as possible, try something like this:

> *"I have been a dedicated, loyal, hard-working employee throughout my career and nothing in my personal life—family obligations, hobbies, or volunteer*

*work—has ever affected my performance. Nor would I
ever expect it to."*

 Q: **What turns you on in your off-hours?**

Many employers subscribe to the theory "If you want something done, give it to a busy person." So, you want to portray yourself as an active, vital individual. Take this opportunity to paint a self-portrait of a well-rounded individual.

 Q: **What do you like to do when you're not at work?**

What do they want to hear?

Talk about both active and passive activities, and be sure to emphasize those activities that may complement your on-the-job duties. For example, if you're applying for a position as a bookstore manager, mentioning that you read three books a week is highly appropriate. Your addiction to helicopter skiing probably isn't (for any job!).

Green light

Shy away from the controversial. A savvy candidate will cite "reading" and "tennis," for example, rather than "bungee jumping" or "picketing abortion clinics." Do you really want your off-hours interests to come between you and the job you're after? Then don't brag about interests that could cause a squeamish employer to envision a prolonged sick leave.

It's generally safe to talk about most sports activities—participating in team sports; coaching children; and indulging in singular activities such as swimming, running, walking, or bicycling. Avoid emphasizing activities that are likely to spark concern or controversy, such as sky diving or hunting.

As a rule, employers like activities that show you are community-minded and people-oriented. Your involvement with the chamber of commerce, Toastmasters, the Rotary Club, or fund raising for charities is likely to earn points. However, consider carefully mentioning any religious or political activities that may alienate the interviewer.

 Red light

Carefully craft your answer so you *don't*:

❶ **Sound like a couch potato.** "I'm a Giants fan. I never miss a game. I also catch every episode of *Buffy the Vampire Slayer*, *ER* and *The X-Files*. And I tape my soap operas every afternoon, so I can catch up on them on the weekends."

❷ **Seem headed for a collapse.** "I play racquetball, coach a softball team, am on the board of directors of the local museum, plan to run for city council this fall, and, in my spare time, attend lectures on Egyptology at the university." (Whew! How will you find the time and energy for work?)

❸ **Boast about dangerous activities.** "I like to challenge myself. Next weekend, I'm signed up for another bungee jump. I need something to keep me pumped up until rugby season starts."

❹ **Bring up controversial interests that may be personally objectionable to the interviewer.** "I'm always on the front lines at Greenpeace demonstrations." Or "I give all my money to the Crusade to Convert the World to (fill in the blank) religion."

Tips for tooting your own horn—without becoming a "blow-hard"

⊃ **Don't get carried away.** Only the most annoying people don't find it difficult to talk about themselves in a flattering way. And that's what you'll be doing on the interview—constantly tooting your own horn, until even you will want to change the tune.

You'll be saying what a great person your friends think you are, what a pleasure your supervisors thought it was to have you on their team, and that there are only a few little adjustments you'd like to make to your personality.

⊃ **Stress the traits companies are looking for.** I mean enthusiasm, confidence, energy, dependability, honesty. Formulate answers that suggest these characteristics. Think about what you would want in an ideal employee if you owned a company. Wouldn't you want a problem-solver? A team player? Someone who is enthusiastic about working hard to achieve goals?

⊃ **Be creative.** A friend of mine had to work his way through college. Rather than participate in low- or no-pay internship programs or extracurricular activities, he pumped gas and stocked supermarket shelves during the summer. These "menial" positions were in no way related to the career he was studying for—publishing. And to compound things, publishing is a very internship-oriented field. Many companies like to hire candidates who have spent their summers fetching coffee for editors and art directors.

My friend knew there would be searching questions about how he had spent his summer vacations from his Ivy League interviewer. So he was ready with this response:

"I wish I'd had more time to write for the school paper. Whenever I wasn't studying, I pretty much had to work to pay for college. But I learned a number of things from the jobs I held that most people learn only after they've been in their careers for a while—such as how to work with other people and how to manage my time effectively."

More tips for interview success

- ⊃ **Shape your responses to the position.** Learn as much as you can about the position for which you are interviewing—before you get to the interview. When you talk about your own accomplishments, skills, and experience, talk in terms of the requirements of *that* job—and the goals of *that* company.

- ⊃ **Always think in terms of what—and why.** As you talk about your accomplishments—or failures—stress the positive lessons you've learned that you've already applied or plan to apply in your next position.

- ⊃ **Don't exaggerate.** Your accomplishments and responsibilities should speak for themselves. If you felt you lacked opportunities to make a mark in the past, say so. If you bend the truth, there are too many ways a savvy interviewer can find you out. Don't learn the hard way—it will probably cost you the job!

- ⊃ **Don't appear desperate...**even if you've been terminated from your previous job! But don't come across as smug, either. Concentrate on expressing your genuine interest and enthusiasm for the opportunities offered by the job on offer—such as more responsibility, more knowledge, and more money.

- ⊃ **Avoid the negative.** You want the interviewer to associate as few negative words or feelings with you as possible.

- ⊃ **Make the best of your current position.** Let the interviewer know you may still be able to find some of the things you're looking for in your current position.

You want to convey the impression that you are a positive worker who tries to make the best of any situation. And again, you're trying not to appear too desperate. Some interviewers will equate "desperate" with "cheap to hire."

➲ **Build a vocabulary of action words.** The following words are strong and positive. If you use them consistently in your resume, interviews, and follow-up letters, they should leave a lasting impression in the interviewer's mind.

Take a few moments to review these words each day, even after you're off the interview circuit. In very little time, they'll find their way into your everyday speaking and writing.

Words that pack a professional punch

Ability	Charted	Decreased
Accelerated	Communicated	Delivered
Accomplished	Compared	Designed
Accurate	Compiled	Detected
Achieved	Completed	Determined
Adjusted	Conceived	Developed
Administered	Conceptualized	Directed
Advised	Conducted	Discovered
Analyzed	Consolidated	Disproved
Approved	Constructed	Distributed
Arranged	Consulted	Edited
Assisted	Controlled	Effective
Built	Coordinated	Eliminated
Calculated	Counseled	Energy
Capable	Created	Enlarged

Enthusiasm	Maintained	Reported
Established	Managed	Represented
Evaluated	Modified	Researched
Examined	Monitored	Responsible
Excelled	Motivated	Restored
Expanded	Negotiated	Reviewed
Focus	Obtained	Revised
Formulated	Operated	Scheduled
Founded	Ordered	Selected
Generated	Organized	Served
Guided	Performed	Sold
Headed	Persuaded	Solved
Identified	Planned	Streamlined
Implemented	Prepared	Strengthened
Improved	Presented	Studied
Increased	Prided	Supervised
Initiated	Processed	Supplied
Inspected	Produced	Systematic
Installed	Proficiency	Taught
Instituted	Programmed	Tested
Instructed	Promoted	Thorough
Interpreted	Proposed	Trained
Introduced	Provided	Translated
Invented	Purchased	Updated
Justified	Recommended	Urgency
Launched	Reduced	Utilized
Lectured	Referred	Vital
Led	Reorganized	Won
Made	Replaced	Wrote

Chapter Nine

Innocent? Hardly. Illegal? Maybe.

As the head of recruiting for a rather large company, a friend of mine spent weeks at a time interviewing scores of candidates for a wide variety of openings. With so much practice, she became very good at identifying unsuitable candidates in minutes—and "releasing" the unsuspecting person with a simple, "Thanks for stopping by" before the interview even got underway!

Here's how it worked. On greeting a young applicant for a field sales position one morning, my friend asked, "How are you?" The applicant immediately began whining about the fact that it was raining and she had a run in her stocking.

This was a cue to my friend. She turned to her and, feigning embarrassment, said, "Oh! Are you here to apply for that field sales position? I'm sorry. We forgot to call. We filled the position yesterday. But we'll keep you in mind for other, similar positions that come along. Thanks for stopping by."

Don't "throwaway" your chances

This story demonstrates a fact that few candidates realize: There is no such thing as an innocent or "throwaway" question. You are being judged from the moment the interviewer sees you (or hears you on the telephone) until the instant you are offered the job (or escorted out of the building). Many interviewers use these questions as "icebreakers," believing that they give a false, informal impression of "let's just chat, shall we?" and lead candidates to drop their interview guard. Some interviewees, dismissed after only a few minutes, belatedly discover that these innocent questions "ice-picked" their chance for the job.

Following are just a few to be prepared for.

How are you today?

Did you have any trouble finding us?

What do they want to hear?

You're doing just fine, thank you. And no, you didn't have any trouble at all! That's because (don't admit to this, just do it) you took the time to get directions from the interviewer's assistant.

Again, it all comes down to being positive. I'm not suggesting that you plaster an idiot grin on your face and go on like a "Stepford" employee. But I do urge you to make every effort not to let anything negative (even the crummy weather!) enter into any part of your interaction with the interviewer.

Since my recruiter friend told me his little story, I know I pay much more attention to the answers candidates give to these little "throwaway" questions.

Over the years, I've taken to asking some out-of-the-blue questions of job candidates. And according to what I read in human resources journals, I'm not at all out of the ordinary.

Many interviewers will try to lure you away from the "standard" interview questions. By now, these questions have become clichés. You've memorized the correct answers to each one, just as if you came into possession of a "stolen" exam. The real test is in how you answer those questions that come from out of the blue.

Covey or King?

 What's the last book you read?

What do they want to hear?

What someone chooses to read speaks volumes about what kind of a person he or she is. But before you reel off your reading list, consider this. Right or wrong, many interviewers seem to think that people who read nonfiction are more interested in the world about them than fiction readers, who they may believe are looking for an escape.

So rather than talk about the latest thriller you couldn't put down, opt for a popular how-to book. This will demonstrate that you're interested in *The 7 Habits of Highly Effective People* or *The Discipline of Market Leaders,* or generally trying to improve your knowledge and skill as a businessperson.

Freddie or Forrest?

 What's the last movie you saw?

What do they want to hear?

Mention a popular but noncontroversial movie. It won't do you any good to gleefully admit it was *Friday the 13th, Part 86*.

Do you want your taste in foreign films or left-wing documentaries to stand between you and a job? It's much better to stay with a Tom Hanks movie like *Forrest Gump*. (If you insist your preferences shouldn't matter, feel free to discuss your ideas on *Natural Born Killers* or *Pulp Fiction*.)

Tips on avoiding a one-minute interview

- ➲ **No question is a throwaway.** The interview begins the moment you walk in the door (or pick up the telephone). So give careful consideration to all of your answers.

- ➲ **Exhibit the traits employers are looking for.** No matter what you're talking about, exude confidence, enthusiasm, energy and intelligence.

- ➲ **Answer carefully—and noncontroversially.** Why open up a can of worms? You may be inviting the interviewer to "go fishing."

- ➲ **Remember, this is still a job interview,** not a meeting of the local literary society or movie fan club. An answer that helps you get the job is preferable to the one that accurately reflects your literary or cinematic tastes.

Discriminate and eliminate?

In an ideal world, companies and managers would judge every applicant solely on the basis of the skills and experience necessary to perform the job.

But it should come as no surprise that our world is far from ideal. In the real world, many managers and companies discriminate against people of color, people with disabilities, people over the age of 50, even women whom they may simply assume are planning to have children sometime during their future employment!

Few of us can claim to be completely objective when judging other people. But the fact is that you, as a candidate for any job, *do not have to answer* questions related to your race, nationality, marital or financial status—or even a disability if it is unrelated to how well you are able to perform the job.

Illegal—or just "inappropriate"?

If an interviewer is foolish enough to make an issue of your nationality, marital status, or other personal information, should you leap out of your chair and make a citizen's arrest right there in the interview? No.

But you should sit up and take notice. Every state has regulations governing what may and may not be asked of an applicant during the pre-employment (application and interviewing) process. Just asking the wrong question is not illegal in itself. But it may open an employer up to a lawsuit if an otherwise-qualified applicant is passed over for a job based on his or her answer. Few companies are willing to take that chance. So when it comes to "inappropriate" questions, most employers tread lightly.

But regulations don't preclude the subtle techniques some interviewers use to get applicants to volunteer information. As an applicant, it's still up to you to dodge the bullet. The key is knowing when a question is inappropriate—and not surrendering any information that might cost you the job.

Your litmus test

Every question the interviewer asks should pass this test: "Does it have something to do with my current job or the one that I'm applying for?"

Beyond that, it pays to check with your state's Fair Employment Practices Commission for a list of questions considered inappropriate for employers to ask on job applications and during preemployment interviews.

In the meantime, here are some questions that should trigger alarms in your head during even the most "congenial" interview.

Questions about your age

 How old are you?

Age can be a loaded issue for many employers. If you're in your late 40s or 50s, some employers may worry about your energy flagging or your health failing. Don't give them ammunition in the form of a number.

Employers cannot ask for your birth date or about facts that might reveal your age, such as the year you graduated from high school. Interviewers may only state that hiring is subject to verification of legal minimum age requirements and that employees under the age of 18 must provide a work permit.

But age, like race, can be easy to guess. So again, take a positive tack. Play up the benefits of your experience and assure the employer that you have all the vitality for work you had when you were in your 20s. You might say:

"The more I've accomplished, the more effective I've become. When I was just starting out, I was so full of energy I was like a loose cannon. Now I find I can accomplish more in less time because I know where to find the resources I need and how to work effectively with all kinds of people."

Variations

➲ *When were you born?*

➲ *When did you graduate from high school?*

➲ *When did you graduate from college?*

➲ *Are you near retirement age?*

➲ *Aren't you a little young to be seeking a job with this much responsibility?*

➲ *Aren't you a little too old for a fast-changing company such as ours?*

Questions about your marital/family status

 Are you single, married, separated, divorced?

Often an interviewer's bias is not overt. Many interviewers use subtle ploys designed to get you to volunteer just the information that they may use to disqualify you from the running.

You may be married with children—and proud of it. But resist the temptation to whip out the latest pictures from Walt

Disney World. Why? After all, what could seem more innocent than chitchatting about your fiancé, spouse, or kids? What's the harm in letting an employer know about your tentative plan for having a child within a year?

Maybe there's no harm in it. But then again, you never know how an interviewer may interpret your answers. If you're planning to have a child within a year, for example, an interviewer may wonder whether you will begin to curtail your hours at work. If you're engaged to be married, he might assume that you'll be so wrapped up in wedding plans that your attention won't be focused on the job at hand.

Interviewers may not ask about your marital status or plans for marriage or for having children. If you already have children, you're not obliged to reveal their ages or the arrangements you've made for childcare. In many states, married women are not required to give an employer their maiden name—unless they've worked under another name at previous companies listed on their resume.

Meeting the interviewer halfway

Rather than simply refusing to answer a question—and creating bad feelings between you and the interviewer—you may find it helpful to confront what you believe might be the employer's concerns about your situation. For example, if the interviewer keeps digging for information about whether you have children, or plan to, he may be concerned about your commitment to the job. You might respond by saying something like:

> *"I sense that you are concerned about my ability to be here on a regular basis to put in the work necessary to meet deadlines. Just let me assure you that I have always been a reliable worker who's committed to*

getting the job done well and on time. In fact, in my last position, I was never late to work once and I consistently completed all projects ahead of deadline."

See? Without answering any questions about children or family plans, you addressed the real issue—the employer's concern about your commitment to your job.

Variations

- *What do you think caused your divorce?*
- *Why have you never married?*
- *Were you ever married?*
- *Do you intend to marry?*
- *Do you live alone?*
- *Do you have any children?*
- *What was your maiden name?*
- *Is that the last name you were born with?*
- *Do you prefer to be called Miss, Ms., or Mrs.?*
- *Are you a single parent?*
- *How many dependents are you responsible for?*
- *Who's the boss in your family?*
- *What kind of work does your spouse do?*
- *How much time do you spend with your family?*
- *What do you think makes a happy marriage?*
- *Tell me about your children.*
- *Do you have a good relationship with your children?*
- *Do you have any children not living with you?*

- Do you live with your parents?
- What childcare arrangements have you made for your children?
- My darn kids seem to pick up every bug that comes around. Yours, too?
- My wife (husband) hates me working on weekends. What about yours?
- Do you practice birth control?
- Are you pregnant?
- Do you intend to have children?
- Will travel be a burden on your family?
- Are you a family man (woman)?

Questions about your ethnic origin

 What's your nationality?

When you meet, you can't stop an interviewer from drawing conclusions about your lineage from the color of your skin, eyes, or hair. But never surrender that information over the telephone—or hand over a photograph of yourself before you accept a job.

Employers may not ask about your ancestry, descent, parentage, or nationality—or that of your parents or spouse. It's okay to volunteer that you're proficient in a language other than English, but the interviewer cannot ask you how you learned to read, write, or speak those languages.

Let's say your last name is "obviously" Italian. When you greet the interviewer, he remarks, "Rutigliano. That's Italian, isn't it?" What do you do? Just smile politely—and don't answer at all. It is quite possible that the interviewer meant absolutely no offense.

If the interviewer still doesn't get the hint and continues to allude to your Italian heritage, you might say, "I really don't see what my ancestry has to do with my application for this job." If you try to handle the situation diplomatically, you can stay on the interviewer's "good" side.

If an employer tries to pressure you into submitting a photograph of yourself to accompany your job application, simply say, "I don't have a suitable photograph available at this time. Of course, if I'm offered this job, I'd be happy to have one taken."

The Federal Immigration Reform and Control Act of 1986 prohibits employers from hiring "aliens"—people who are not properly authorized to work in this country. *Once you have accepted the offer*, you will be required to document your right to work by surrendering one of the following:

- ⊃ A United States passport.
- ⊃ A green card.
- ⊃ A combination of a birth certificate or social security card and a driver's license.

Variations

- ⊃ *Hmm, that's a ___ (Italian, Greek, etc.) name, isn't it?*
- ⊃ *What language do you speak at home?*
- ⊃ *Where are your parents from?*
- ⊃ *Where were you born?*
- ⊃ *Where were your parents born?*
- ⊃ *What languages do your parents speak?*

- ➲ *What do your parents do?*
- ➲ *Were your parents born in this country?*
- ➲ *Were you born in this country?*
- ➲ *What kind of accent is that?*
- ➲ *What languages do you speak?*
- ➲ *Are you bilingual?*

Questions about your sexual preference

 What's your sexual orientation?

"I'm sorry. I don't intend to discuss that."

Variations

- ➲ *Are you straight?*
- ➲ *Are you gay?*
- ➲ *Are you a lesbian?*
- ➲ *Do you date other men?*
- ➲ *Do you date other women?*
- ➲ *Do you have any roommates?*
- ➲ *Do you belong to any gay or lesbian groups?*

Questions about your religious preference

 Are you ___ (Jewish, Christian, Buddhist, etc.)?

Employers may tell you which religious holidays the company observes. But they cannot ask you for any specific information in this area.

If an interviewer presses you to reveal your affiliation, simply say:

> *"I like to keep my religious beliefs separate from my work, and I respect that right in the people with whom I work."*

But if you find yourself dodging too many of these "bullets," maybe you should take a moment to think about whether you want to work for a supervisor who has shown himself to be ignorant and insensitive. If you don't care that he's an insensitive boob—you just want the job—then don't make an issue out of his comments. It's up to you.

Variations

- *What do you do Sunday mornings?*
- *Can you work Friday evenings?*
- *We're a ___ (Christian, Jewish, Muslim) firm. Would that be a problem for you?*
- *Are you a member of any religious group?*
- *What religion do you practice?*
- *Do you tithe?*
- *Are you "born again"?*
- *Do your children go to Sunday School?*
- *Do your children go to Hebrew School?*
- *Do you sing in the church choir?*
- *What church do you belong to?*

➲ *Is there any day of the week on which you can't work?*

➲ *Will working on weekends be a problem for you?*

➲ *What religious holidays will you need to take?*

➲ *What organizations do you belong to?*

Questions about your health and disabilities

 Do you have any physical problems?

Interviewers may only ask about a physical or mental disability that will directly affect your performance on the job.

Your general physical health is not fair game, although you may be asked to take a physical examination after you receive an offer. The outcome of this examination must be related to essential functions of the job—so the employer has the right to condition the offer on the results.

Employers may *not* ask about whether you have:

➲ An existing mental condition.

➲ Received workers' compensation.

➲ Problems with alcohol or drugs.

➲ HIV, AIDS, or AIDS-related syndrome.

A word about AIDS

This is still an area of concern for employers. Although new laws and regulations will likely be written, currently HIV infection, AIDS, and AIDS-related medical conditions are considered "disabilities" under the Federal Americans with Disabilities Act.

If you test positive for HIV or AIDS (or any other disability) in a pre-employment medical examination, the employer cannot use that information as grounds for withdrawing the offer—unless the extent of the illness substantially inhibits your ability to do the job or poses a reasonable threat to the safety of others in the workplace.

Variations

- ➲ *Do you have any health problems?*
- ➲ *How many days were you sick last year?*
- ➲ *Do you spend a lot on prescriptions?*
- ➲ *Can you read the fine print on this form?*
- ➲ *How's your back?*
- ➲ *Is your hearing good?*
- ➲ *Are you physically fit?*
- ➲ *Were you ever denied health insurance?*
- ➲ *Were you ever denied life insurance?*
- ➲ *When were you last in the hospital?*
- ➲ *When did you last consult a doctor?*
- ➲ *Do you have a doctor you see regularly?*
- ➲ *Are you handicapped?*
- ➲ *Have you ever filed a workman's compensation claim?*

Other personal questions

 What organizations are you a member of?

Think carefully about your answer to this question. An employer can ask about (and should only be interested in) your membership in organizations, professional societies, or other associations considered important to your performance on the job.

It's a good idea to leave out the names of any organizations that might provide "clues" to your race, religious creed, color, national origin, ancestry, gender, or disability.

 Have you ever gone bankrupt?

A prospective employer may only ask what you're currently earning.

Your current or past assets, liabilities, or credit rating are not fair game. This includes whether you own a home or any information about a past bankruptcy or garnishment of wages (except when permitted by federal and state laws governing credit-related information). Again, it's wise to consult specific guidelines in your state.

Variations

- ⮑ *Do you own or rent your home?*
- ⮑ *Do you have any outside income?*
- ⮑ *Do you earn any money from hobbies or investments?*

 What was your record in the military?

If you have served in the military and want to bring to light the skills and knowledge you gained from that experience that are relevant to the job you're applying for, go ahead. But be aware that you're *not* required to give the dates of your military service or the type of discharge you received.

A dishonorable discharge from the military or an arrest that did not result in a conviction does not mean your professional life is over. In the majority of cases, these facts should remain in your past.

Be aware, however, that regulations do differ from state to state and from industry to industry. For example, under the Federal Deposit Insurance Act, banks are prohibited from hiring individuals convicted of any crime involving dishonesty or breach of trust, even if the conviction is more than seven years old.

Variation

➲ *What kind of discharge did you receive?*

 Have you ever been arrested?

Unless you're applying for a position as a police officer or with the Department of Justice, a prospective employer is not entitled to know whether you've been arrested—unless the arrest resulted in a conviction.

In some states, employers may only ask about felonies, not misdemeanors. If you have a record, do some research.

So what do you do?

Over the past 25 years, there has been a plethora of lawsuits charging employers with discriminatory hiring practices, yet inappropriate questions still are commonly asked during interviews.

This is particularly true of interviews by hiring managers, who may not be up on legal issues. If you're asked an inappropriate question, you have three choices:

❶ You can be a constitutionalist and refuse, on principle, to answer—even if you'd come up smelling like a rose if you did.

❷ You can be a pragmatist and provide answers you feel wouldn't hurt you, while you tactfully sidestep questions you think could hurt you.

❸ You can be a little of both.

Beware the wily interviewer

Most interviewers who are trying to get at information that is considered inappropriate won't be obvious. Here's a case of subtle discrimination.

After making it through three interviews for a job at one of the big tobacco companies, a friend of mine thought she was "in." But during her final interview, the interviewer offered her a cigarette. She replied, "No, thanks. I don't smoke."—without realizing that she had inadvertently said no to the job as well!

Notice the subtlety. The interviewer never asked, "Are you a smoker?" or "Do you smoke?" Turning down an applicant because she refused to engage in an unhealthy activity might put the company on questionable legal and public relations ground. But by getting her to volunteer the information, the interviewer had what he needed to disqualify her from the running.

(When I heard this story, I couldn't help but wish she had answered, "No, thanks. I don't smoke during interviews." Perfectly true—and nearly as coy as the interviewer's gambit!)

What to do after the fact

If an interviewer has asked you questions not related to the job on offer, and you believe you weren't hired based on your refusal to answer or the information you did provide, you might have grounds for charging the employer with discrimination.

The operative word here is "might." The burden of proof is on you. You will have to prove that the questions were asked for the purpose of discriminating among applicants. For example, if the manager asking all those questions about Italian ancestry subsequently hired another Italian, you wouldn't have much of a claim, despite the fact that you were asked inappropriate questions.

If you do think that you have grounds for a charge of discrimination, you should file your charges simultaneously with the appropriate state agency and the federal government's Equal Employment Opportunity Commission (EEOC). The EEOC generally will wait until the state agency has conducted an investigation, then conduct an investigation of its own.

As you might expect, the wheels of government agencies can creak at their own slow pace. In fact, you might not hear anything for years! Even then, an agency will only determine whether there is reason to believe your charge is true. Therefore, if you are anxious for justice, you should request that the EEOC issue you a notice 180 days after you file your charge.

If you're in the right

If the EEOC determines that your complaint is valid, it will first attempt to mediate the dispute between you and the employer. If an agreement can't be reached, the Commission will either file its own suit or issue you a letter giving you the right to sue the employer. You must file your suit within 90 days of receiving such a letter.

Say that you win your lawsuit. Don't expect to receive a colossal jury award. The most you'll probably get from the employer is the equivalent of a year's salary.

One last word...

None of the information or advice in this chapter should be taken as legal advice. I am not an attorney. If you feel a prospective employer is guilty of discrimination, your first step should be to contact the appropriate government agencies, as well as an attorney, to accurately assess your rights and options under federal law and the laws and regulations in your state and industry.

Tips for fending off illegal questions

- ⮂ **Know your rights.** Do some research to find out what questions are out of bounds in your particular state, industry or profession.

- ⮂ **Don't open the door for the interviewer.** Let him get it himself! That is, don't bring up subjects you don't want to talk about. If you do, the interviewer is likely to ask what would otherwise have been illegal questions—if you hadn't opened the door first.

- ⮂ **Change the subject.** If you feel that the interviewer is asking you questions that shouldn't be asked, the first step is to try to shrug them off and change the direction of the conversation.

- ⮂ **Give the benefit of the doubt.** After all, you are here because you want the job. So it's up to you to weigh your personal reactions to certain searching questions against your desire to have this job. Many hiring managers may not realize they are in the wrong. Give them the benefit of the doubt.

- ⮂ **Warn the interviewer—subtly.** Tell the interviewer in a nonthreatening way that you know the questions he or she is asking are inappropriate. This should deliver the message that you know your rights and aren't willing to be a victim of discrimination.

- ⮂ **End the interview.** If the interviewer refuses to back off, end the interview quickly. After all, would you really want to work at a company or for a person capable of such narrow-minded attitudes? If you think you have a strong case, look into bringing formal charges against the company and the interviewer.

Chapter Ten

That's a Wrap!

O kay, you've made it this far, you *must* have the job by now. Anyway, there's absolutely no way to screw it up at this point, right?

Don't be so quick to relax. The closing questions of an interview should be handled with care. In short, there are still likely to be some tough questions ahead. Here goes.

Planes, trains, and automobiles

 Are you willing to travel?

What do they want to hear?

Yes, of course you are. Your family understands the demands of your career and is supportive when you need to spend some time away from home. Does that mean you want to be away three weeks out of four? Probably not. Unless you are unwilling to travel at all, don't let this question cost you the job. (If the job requires far more travel than you are prepared for, what are you doing on the interview? And if the heavy travel requirements are a complete shock, why didn't you learn about them beforehand?)

The more travel is an inherent part of the job, the more likely the interviewer will ask this question *early* in the process, so as to immediately eliminate home-bound candidates.

 Are you willing to relocate?

What do they want to hear?

If you really are, say so. "Absolutely. In fact, I would look forward to the chance to live elsewhere and experience a different lifestyle and meet new people."

If you're not, say so. "Well, not unless the job is so terrific that it would be worth uprooting my family and leaving my relatives and friends. Does this position require a move? I'm obviously very interested in it, so I might consider relocating."

 May I contact your current employer?

Why do people ask this question? You probably will feel like saying, "Sure, after you give me this job and I don't have to worry about getting canned because I've been out looking for another job."

But you'll sound better saying: "Sure you can—after we come to an agreement. I think it's best if they hear about this from me first."

May I contact your references?

What do they want to hear?

Of course. Tell the interviewer that you will get back to him or her with a list of references that afternoon or, if it is already afternoon, the very next day.

Does this stalling make you seem unprepared? Shouldn't you go into the interview with the list ready to hand over to the interviewer?

Frankly, in the world of interviews, stalling for a little time before giving references is SOP (standard operating procedure). The reason you want to wait is so you can tell your prospective references that a call might be coming from Mr. Krueger of Trikadekaphobia, Inc. If your references are indeed going to say wonderful things about you, they should be prepared to do so.

Caveat: Employers are growing more reluctant to provide references because of a rise in the number of claims of defamation and misrepresentation. Because job references are partially privileged communications, it's a good idea to try to get an inside line on what is being said about you to a prospective employer. As an applicant, you may be able to approach a current or former employer to work out a narrative job reference that is accurate and amenable to both of you. With your consent and involvement, former employers may be more willing to discuss your strengths and weaknesses and the circumstances surrounding your departure in a positive light.

 Is there anything else about you I should know?

What do they want to hear?

You might not think you have anything else left to say—but you'd better have! This is your chance—on a silver platter—to close the sale. You'd be a fool to walk away from it.

Develop a short answer to this question, one that plays upon your strengths, accomplishments, skills, and areas of knowledge. For example:

"Mr. Krueger, I think we've covered everything. But I want to re-emphasize the key strengths that I would bring to this position.

➲ **Experience.** The job I'm currently in is quite similar to this one, and I would be excited by the chance to apply what I've learned at WidgetLand to working for your company.

➲ **Management skills.** I run a department almost equal in size to this one. I'm a fair and effective supervisor.

➲ **A record of success.** I've won two prestigious industry awards. I would bring that creativity here.

➲ **Enthusiasm.** I am very excited about the prospect of working with you here at Trikadekaphobia. When do you expect to make a decision?

This type of answer should underline the points that you have been trying to make throughout the entire interview. By ending with a question, you ask Mr. Krueger to take some action. This is an effective selling technique that should give you a good indication of your chances of getting the job.

Variations

➲ *Why should I hire you?*

➲ *If you were me, would you hire you?*

Keys to wrapping up a successful interview

➲ **Be prepared to ask questions.** Remember, an interview is a two-way street. Your job is to find out if the company, the industry and the hiring manager are right for you. Don't be shy about asking the interviewer some rather tough questions of your own.

➲ **Don't ask about time off.** At least not before you're offered the job.

➲ **Don't ask about salary or benefits.** Wait until you are offered the job. You don't want money to be a factor when the interviewer is considering whether you are the best person for the job.

➲ **Prepare a closing argument.** This should briefly summarize your strengths, skills, and accomplishments, and underline those that the interviewer has already told you are key to the job.

➲ **Don't give out the names of your references.** Instead, take the time to notify these people that they may hear from your prospective employer and let them know what you want them to stress (or leave out).

Money talks

No one likes to talk about money during an interview. It seems "indelicate," somehow. But that doesn't mean you should avoid it completely. Just remember that timing is everything.

My own rule of thumb is simple: Don't discuss dollars and cents until after you've convinced the interviewer that you're the best person for the job.

That's why I've relegated the first question on salary to near the end of the final chapter. Until you've made it over all the other interview hurdles, the interviewer is still assessing your ability. And he or she is probably still seeing other contenders as well—some whose talent may come cheaper than yours.

But even if an interviewer tries to pressure you into naming a specific number early in the game, avoid committing yourself. Instead, name a very broad range. You might say, "I believe a fair wage for this kind of position would be something like $30,000 to $40,000."

Be sure the bottom end of that range is no less than the minimum salary you would be willing to accept for the position.

Once the employer has made his decision, you're in a much stronger bargaining position.

What sort of salary are you looking for?

What do they want to hear?

You must have a pretty good idea of what your particular market will bear. If you don't know the high and low ends in your area (city and state) and industry, do some research. Make sure you know whether these figures represent just dollars or a compensation "package" that may include insurance, retirement programs, and other value-added benefits.

If you're a woman, make sure you know what men are making doing the same job. You're bound to find a discrepancy. But you should request and expect to earn an equivalent salary, regardless of what women predecessors may have earned.

Even if you've been out of a job for months, this is not the time or place to let your desperation show, so avoid gushing,

"Gee, this job sounds so gosh-darned wonderful I can't believe you're going to pay me anything! Just give me an office and a phone and I'll work for the sheer fun of it!"

I'm worth it!

Have confidence in your own worth. By this time, you've worked hard to sell the interviewer on your value as a future employee. Just remind him of what he's already decided.

Harry is a friend of mine who is not only eminently qualified, but also a heck of a good interview, and he knows it.

So, when a recruiter called Harry with a job lead that sounded perfect for him—but paid less than he was making—Harry told her: "I want that job. Send me on the interview. After they've met me, they'll be willing to pay me what I want."

It sounds cocky, but Harry knew what he was doing. During the interview process, he studiously avoided the subject of salary. When the interviewer finally asked, "What would it take to get you over here?" Harry showed his cards.

"I understand the job has a top salary of $40,000," he said. When the interviewer affirmed that, he went on: "Well, I would need more than that. I came here because the job sounded terrific. In fact, the job description Gretchen gave me, and which you've just elaborated on, has my name written all over it."

To make a long story short, Harry got the salary he wanted because he had already sold himself. If he had asked for the same money earlier in the interview, he probably would have been out of the running.

What if your initial offer is not accepted? Then it's time to negotiate.

The salary you're asking for is near the top of the range for this job. Why should we pay you this much?

What do they want to hear?

Remind the employer of the cost savings and other benefits he'll enjoy when you come on board. Pull out your specifics again, if necessary. For example, you might say:

> "I was able to cut my previous employer's expenses by 10 percent by negotiating better deals with vendors. I think it's reasonable to expect that any additional salary we agree to would be offset by savings I could bring the company."

You've come to an agreement, and the last piece of business before you start your new job.

 When can you start?

What do they want to hear?

If you've been laid off or fired, you can start immediately, of course.

But if you're still working for someone else, you must give at least two weeks' notice to your employer—more if you are leaving a position in which you had considerable responsibility.

As eager as you may be to get started on this new job, I know I don't have to remind you that it's never wise to burn bridges. You never know when you might have to cross one of them again! So be as accommodating as you can. For example, offer to help find and train your replacement.

If it will be several weeks before you can assume your new responsibilities full-time, offer to begin studying literature or files in your off-hours. Or come into the office in the evening or on a weekend to meet members of the staff and begin to familiarize yourself with the lay of the land. You might even be called on to attend a company event or seminar.

Red light

Although it may reflect your true feelings about the job, saying you "aren't sure" when you can start implies to me you "aren't sure" about taking the job.

Don't ever admit you can't start for several weeks because you want to take a vacation. I can empathize with someone who feels the need to "recover" from a bitter job experience before punching the clock at a new one, but there's just something that sticks in my craw about such an answer. Perhaps it's feeling that you're already putting your own needs above mine—maybe it's a real hardship for me to wait four weeks. Maybe it's my own idiosyncrasy, but I *really* hate to hear about someone planning a vacation before starting to work for me.

Q: Is there anything that will inhibit you from taking this job if offered?

What do they want to hear?

"Absolutely not."

The interviewer is attempting to do everything in his power to ascertain whether you'll accept the job if offered and actually show up on the start date. But there is no way he can guarantee either. All he can hope to do is give you another opportunity to voice a previously hidden concern—too small a salary, a poor benefits package, a lousy cubicle, reporting to too many people, inadequate support, unrealistic sales or profit expectations, etc.

 ## Are you considering any other offers right now?

What do they want to hear?

This is another "closing" question I like to ask early in the process so I know what I'm up against. Of course, this is presuming that an honest answer is good for *you*, which, frankly, it probably isn't. Unless you believe the interviewer will respond positively to such an admission, you should play your cards very close to the vest. You probably gain nothing by admitting you have other irons in the fire, so why stir up the coals?

Apres-interview etiquette

Once you step out from under the bright lights and shake hands with the interviewer, it will probably take all the composure you can muster not to kick up your heels and run out of the office.

But in your hurry, don't forget that the process is not quite over. Whether you're waiting by the phone for word or off to your next "ordeal," there are a few standard rules of etiquette you should follow.

➲ **Ask when the hiring decision will be made.** If you don't get word by then, it's perfectly acceptable to call the employer to inquire about the status of the position.

➲ **Write a thank you note.** Make it short and sweet. Thank the interviewer for taking the time to meet with you. Then restate your interest in the company and the position and find a way to remind the interviewer of how you can use your skill and experience to address one of the key requirements of the job.

Type it in business-style and be sure there are no typographical or spelling errors. A good example appears below.

Remember that if you met with more than one interviewer, you should send thank you letters to each person with whom you talked.

Dear Mr. Jones,

Thank you for taking the time to discuss the position of purchasing manager with me yesterday. It was a pleasure meeting you and learning more about Start Up Co.

During our meeting, you mentioned that you'll be shopping around for a new computerized materials management system soon. During my years at Consolidated, Inc., I reviewed and worked with a number of these systems, and I have a few thoughts about which ones might work best for you. I'd be happy to share my thoughts with you at any time.

Again, thank you for your consideration. I look forward to hearing from you and the possibility of joining your staff.

Sincerely,

Jane Anderson

Tips on wrapping up a winning "package"

➲ **Wait until you receive an offer.** Defer any question of salary that comes up early in the interview with an answer like this: "Colleen in human resources indicated the salary range for this position, and it seems about right to me." Or: "I'd like to know a little bit more about the job responsibilities and the level of expertise you're expecting before I feel comfortable discussing a salary."

➲ **Know your worth.** Remember that the company wants you. They have decided you are the best candidate they have met. This puts you in a position of power. If they balk at your initial salary demand, remind them of a few specific benefits they stand to gain from hiring you.

➲ **Research compensation levels.** Look within your industry and locally—within your city and state. If you don't already know the salary range for the specific position you're considering, find out. You need to go into salary negotiations armed with this information.

➲ **Negotiate the perks.** Make sure you understand the value of all the potential benefits in the salary/benefits package. Benefits can vary widely. Some companies buy employees company cars and club memberships. Others give bonuses or extra time off.

➲ **Go for the top.** If that is more than the company will pay, the interviewer will counter with another offer. Work toward a compromise from there.

➲ **Get it in writing.** Especially if you negotiate a complex, nonstandard salary/benefits package. Be sure you have something in writing—either a letter or memo from the employer, or one you've sent that's been accepted— before you give notice to your current employer.

Finishing touches

➲ **Nourish your network.** If a colleague or former associate referred you to the company or arranged a personal introduction with the interviewer or hiring manager, be sure to drop that person a note of thanks as well.

➲ **Replay the highs—and the lows.** What went well during the interviewing process? What could you have done better? The point is not to berate yourself for what you did or didn't say. You merely want to make sure you keep doing the things that worked—and working on what didn't—so you can ace your next interview.

➲ **Rewrite your resume.** Did the interviewer have any questions that you could clarify through your resume? Did you find yourself talking about accomplishments you forgot to include? If so, now is the time to revise your resume—before you send it out again.

➲ **Keep in touch.** The hiring process can move at a snail's pace in corporate America. Often, the larger the corporation, the slower the pace. So don't panic if a week or two passes before you hear anything. No news may be good news. If time stretches on, it's okay to call to find out if the job has been filled. Use the opportunity to remind the employer of your interest and qualifications.

➲ **Accept—in your own time and on your own terms.** Never accept an offer at the time it is tendered. Take a day or two to think about it. Tell the interviewer when you will announce your decision. If you do decide to refuse the offer, politely tell the employer why you don't feel you can accept the position.

➲ **Congratulate yourself.** You made it through one of life's more stressful experiences with flying colors. You've proven you're a real pro. Now you're on your way.

Index